FIR...
&
MORE WILL BE ...ED.

The Way of Unknowing

HEARTFELT WELCOME

Joe

The Way of Unknowing

Expanding Spiritual Horizons
Through Meditation

John Main

Introduction by
Laurence Freeman

CANTERBURY
PRESS
Norwich

© The World Community for Christian Meditation 2011

This edition published in 2011 by the Canterbury Press Norwich
Editorial office
13–17 Long Lane,
London, EC1A 9PN, UK

Canterbury Press is an imprint of Hymns Ancient & Modern Ltd
(a registered charity)
13A Hellesdon Park Road, Norwich,
Norfolk, NR6 5DR, UK

Published in the United States in 1995 by
The Crossroad Publishing Company

www.canterburypress.co.uk

British Library Cataloguing in Publication data

A catalogue record for this book is available
from the British Library

978 1 84825 118 2

For
Madeleine Simon RCSJ

Contents

Contents

How to Meditate

Sit down. Sit still and upright. Close your eyes lightly. Sit relaxed but alert. Silently, interiorly begin to say a single word. We recommend the prayer-phrase *'maranatha'*. Recite it as four syllables of equal length. Listen to it as you say it, gently but continuously. Do not think or imagine anything – spiritual or otherwise. If thoughts and images come, these are distractions at the time of meditation, so keep returning to simply saying the word. Meditate each morning and evening for between twenty and thirty minutes.

Addresses of meditation centers are on the last page of this book.

Introduction

Every art, including the art of prayer, requires a teacher. No one can absolve another, however, of the personal responsibilities of entering the experience for him or herself. Teachers are facilitators. Literally that means they make it easier for us to do – or become – what by our own resources we might fail to achieve because of discouragement or ignorance.

For many people in both the west and the east John Main has become such a teacher, one who makes it easier to meditate. Meditation groups and centres are now forming in response to his teaching in Asia as well as in Europe, America and Australia. His teaching has inspired many to begin and many to persevere on the journey of meditation. Yet he does not teach that meditation is easy. Simplicity is the essence of his message about meditation and for anyone who can understand that the path to the kingdom is simple, that alone makes it easier.

John Main rediscovered the Christian tradition of meditation after he had become a Benedictine monk. But he first learnt to meditate from an Indian monk. From his monastery and through his travels John Main began the work of teaching meditation which has continued to develop in many and various ways since his death in 1982.

This new book of John Main's richly consistent teaching will serve a double purpose: to encourage and deepen further the pilgrimage of the heart on which people already meditating are engaged; and to introduce people for the first time to the journey which he said it is only necessary to begin. Nothing could better express the wisdom of this teacher than the fact that the same teaching can encourage the proficient and launch the beginner. Simplicity is tested by the unity it creates among all who enter the same journey of faith. It is a journey in which the humble are exalted and those who think they have become experts are brought back to the starting-point. Experience of the kingdom, which is the meaning of meditation, is not bounded by time. It can dawn at any stage of the journey depending upon grace and the disposition of childlikeness of the meditator.

In these short chapters the voice of John Main helps to prepare the reader for this simplicity of the state of pure prayer. Listening attentively to the voice will prepare you for meditation. In the same way the talks which were the first form of these chapters prepared the meditation groups for the silence and stillness of the 'time of the mantra'. This is a book, then, to be read in conjunction with the experience of prayer. It is not about meditation. It is for meditation. And it is a book to throw away, forgetting what it says, when you sit down actually to meditate. But it is a book to pick up again afterwards, to come to a fuller understanding of what the experience of prayer means and to prepare for the next step of the journey – the next meditation.

Because he was a Christian teacher John Main knew and taught that for the Christian Christ in the Spirit is always the teacher. He teaches us in many ways, however, and appears to us in the manner and form best suited to our needs and capacity at the moment. Scripture acquaints us with our teacher and meditation will send us back to read the Bible with purified and more attentive minds. Communities of faith introduce us to our teacher and meditation groups are becoming real schools of faith throughout the world. Life itself, work, relationships, accidents and designs, all reveal the Lord who is in all events because he is at the centre of each person.

Christ also teaches us through certain of his disciples. John Main said that it was the teacher's first task to get out of the way as soon as possible and so reveal the Lord. In the talks and answers he gives in this collection, you will I hope meet Christ more personally by seeing John Main get out of the way. His manner of teaching was not egocentric. It did not focus attention on his own personality or even his own experience. He taught from experience but in order to lead the listener to his or her own experience.

John Main will have successfully taught us if his words lead us not to think about him or even his compassionate, humourous, incisive wisdom – but to the stillness in which we know God.

Christian Meditation Centre   LAURENCE FREEMAN OSB
London
March 1989

In Reverence in our Heart

The most important thing to know about meditation is *how* to meditate. It is also important, I suppose, to know *why* you should meditate, but in the first place you must know what to do. Let me remind you of this again so that you are as clear as possible in your minds about it. Choose a place that is as quiet as you can find. As far as posture is concerned, the basic rule is to sit with your spine upright. Sit down, either on the floor or in an upright chair, and keep your spine as erect as possible. Close your eyes gently. To meditate you need to take a word and the word I suggest to you is *maranatha*. Simply, gently repeat that word in silence in your heart, in the depths of your being, and continue repeating it. Listen to it as a sound. Say it; articulate it in silence, clearly, but listen to it as a sound. If you can, you must meditate every morning and every evening. I think it is true to say that you will never learn to meditate unless you do meditate every morning and every evening of every day. You need simply to put that time-slot aside.

Now what does it mean to us as Christians to meditate? Consider this advice from the first letter of St Peter. He says to the early Christians, 'Do not be perturbed but hold the Lord Christ in reverence in your hearts' (1 Pet. 3:15). There is the essence of the first Christian understanding of what it means to be a Christian. They knew, as we know, that we live in a world of change, of confusion, indeed very often of chaos. And the early Christians also knew that this change, confusion and chaos were not only to be found outside of themselves but inside of themselves. Indeed they knew, as we know, that most of the external confusion in the world is caused directly by the internal confusion in each of us. They knew that the constant human challenge is to find harmony, order and peace. They

1

knew that the primary challenge is to find that in ourselves, in our own hearts. They knew, too, that if we can find that order, peace and harmony, and that discipline, within ourselves then, although much of the external confusion will inevitably remain, it will no longer have any power over us. Jesus spoke of it like this: 'The winds, the storms and the rains may come and beat upon that house but it will stand firm because it is founded on rock.' The early Christians knew from their own experience that Christ himself is the rock. He is the rock-like foundation upon which each one of us must build our own lives. They knew from their own experience, as we must know from our own experience, that Christ is the living principle of harmony, of order, of love. They knew, as we must know, that the essential harmony and the essential order can only be based upon love. And they knew, just as we must know, that when we base our lives upon Christ, as rock and foundation, then we are rooted in reality itself. We are then so rooted in essential reality that nothing else has ultimate power over us, not even death itself. Because we are rooted in the eternal love that nothing can destroy.

Now the challenge that each one must face is to find the way to this rock-like foundation. The challenge is to find how each one of us can hold the Lord Christ in reverence in our hearts. So, a little later, St Peter tells us, 'Christ was put to death in the body and brought to life in the Spirit.' This is also what we have to do, no longer basing our lives on desire for things that pass away but, as St Peter puts it, rebuilding our lives on the will of God. For Peter, obeying the will of God is not simply carrying out the Divine Regulations but fully responding to our destiny which is to become alive with the life of God in the Spirit. This is the heart of the Christian message, and it is what we as Christians must learn to communicate to our contemporaries if we are to be faithful to the mission we were given by Jesus.

Alive with the life of God, in the Spirit. This is the importance of our daily meditation. Our daily meditation is nothing less than a return to this fountainhead of life where our spirit becomes wholly immersed in the Spirit of God, wholly alive with his life, wholly loving with his love. We must never be satisfied to settle for less. We must never allow ourselves as Christians to become complacent, mindless or discouraged. St Peter in the same letter tells us to 'Lead an ordered life given to prayer.' He goes on to say that we must keep our love for one another 'at full strength'. But that we can only do if we are fully alive with the life of God. This is the reason for our meditation. To be open to the divine reality that is closer to us than we are to ourselves. The challenge, then, is to live out the reality that Christ has achieved for each one of us, in each one of us. To live our lives founded on the rock that is Christ, alive with his Spirit, alive with the spirit of love. Our daily meditation and our faithfulness to it is simply our return and our openness to this supreme reality.

When we look at the New Testament, at least when we look at it with eyes enlightened by the spirit of Christ burning in our hearts, we cannot but become intoxicated, amazed at the sheer wonder of the destiny that is given to each of us. But, we must always remember that the condition of being open to this, and of responding to our destiny, is always simplicity, poverty of spirit. It means we are invited by the same destiny to leave behind all complexity, all desire to possess God or to possess spiritual knowledge and to tread the narrow way of dispossession. We require faithfulness. We learn to be faithful by being simply faithful to the daily times of meditation and, during the meditation, to the saying of the mantra.

From your experience of this specific fidelity, consider St Peter again:

You must lead an ordered and sober life given to prayer. Above all keep your love for one another at full strength because love cancels out innumerable sins. Be hospitable to one another without complaining. And whatever gift each of you may have received, use it in the service of one another like good stewards dispensing the grace of God in its varied forms. Are you a speaker? Speak as if you uttered oracles of God. Do you give service? Give it as in the strength which God supplies. And in all things, so act that the glory may be God's through Jesus Christ, for to him belong glory and power for ever and ever. (1 Pet. 4:7–11)

3

We fulfil our destiny, which in Christian language is our vocation, by glorifying God in all we do. But this is only realistically possible if we glorify God in all we are. Meditation brings us to that unity of being fully alive in which we glorify God, reflect God's own glory back to him, by simply being who we are, *now*.

God's Two Silences

The increasing godlessness of so much modern consciousness has raised an urgent concern about the survival of humanity, not only of the race but of the *humanity* of the race. Rather than merely denouncing atheism, faith needs to seek a contemporary means to meet the godless, in sympathy and compassion. This means discovering an experience in common. We can find this common experience in the silence of God. Differently interpreted as it may be, it remains a common ground in which the word of faith can be transmitted.

As Christians today we need to reflect deeply on the notion of the silence of God. Before man heard the Word, the Word was already in God. We read this in the Gospel of John. And when the Word was spoken it became the revelation of a mystery that had been shrouded in darkness and silence from the beginning of the ages. There is a real sense in which our personal call to know and to serve God is of the same order. Even before God calls us to knowledge of him and before he calls us to serve him, God already knows and loves us in our mother's womb. Here, already, is part of the mystery of silence in which we all unconsciously participate. Underlying the human encounter with God is this extraordinary mystery that God knows us from the very beginning. He calls us from the very beginning speaking the Word when the time is ripe. So the silence of God is, from the first human experience of it, pregnant with love, pregnant with power. When the Word is spoken, it is a word of revelation, bringing to birth the wonder of God's love, revealed in human bodies, minds and hearts.

It is wonderful, therefore, but not surprising, that a very important aspect of meditation is its silence. It means that we can be there to listen, to hear with open attention. And it is a

5

very fertile silence that we encounter in our meditation, one that is vibrant with God's presence, vibrant with his love; vibrant in summoning us beyond ourselves, beyond our self-limitations and revealing to us the unimaginable potentiality revealed once we ally ourselves to this enlightening power of love.

There is also another silence of God that we could describe as his testing of us. It is a magisterial silence. It is silence that purifies us and to purify us he allows us to remain in this silence of absence and loss; to experience what it is to be cut off from a sense of his reality; to experience what it is to be cut off from the sense of his presence. It is a sense-less silence and faith is forced to greater depths by senselessness in any form. Part of the discipline of meditation is that we learn to be open to both of these silences. In our meditation we enter into this dual aspect of God's silence.

There is, firstly, the revelation that comes as we consciously enter more deeply into the presence. We move into a silence that is increasingly sensed to be an infinite silence. So, we feel a real sense of mystery as we penetrate into its depths and come to understand that the silence needs to be infinite in order to contain the infinite presence of God. Our experience of this silence is one of expansion as our spirit opens up into infinite realms of being. Now sometimes we long to possess this silence. It is so mysterious. It is so holy. As we all soon learn from our experience, we cannot possess God; nor can we possess his silence. We must be content to enter into it when he summons us.

We must be unfearfully prepared for the other silence too, the silence of loss. Sometimes then we long for the silence to be broken so that we may hear the direct Word of God spoken to us in our heart, but experience teaches us that the full wordlessness of this abyss of silence is itself an extraordinary communication. We should not underestimate how seriously each of us is invited to receive this communication of silence and indeed how urgently we need it. We live in a very unsilent world. We live in a world that is so full of bombarding fore-ground and background noise that we hear everything at once and listen to nothing. And yet each one of us is called into the state of prayer, of pure attention, of expansion of spirit in the eternal silence of God.

Now this second sort of silence, when God seems to have withdrawn his presence, is also a reality. It is one where we are left with no sense of his being but only with the sense of his wholesale withdrawal from our world, from our consciousness. We learn over and over again in meditation that we must never become possessive. It is true that it is wonderful when we do have the sense of God's infinity filling us with an infinite calm, a profound sense of wonder. This is a wonderful gift but it is not one that we must either seek or seek to possess, or to confect. One of the things we learn through meditation as we mature, as we go further along the path, is to be equally content with either of these forms of silence, with the infinite sense of his presence as with the finite sense of his absence. It is harder for us at the beginning because when we start to meditate we haven't learned much detachment. We haven't reached the stage where we can be equally content with absence as with presence, and anyway we are always looking for our meditation to satisfy us. We are always looking to prove to ourselves that it works, that now we know God, now we have learned to live in his presence. But the purpose of the second form of silence, his absence, is to purify us so that we learn to love God selflessly as he loves us (and himself). He teaches us to be strong in love, strong in fidelity and to ensure that we love God *for* himself and *in* himself and not only for any manifestation of his presence that satisfies us.

One of the things that we have to learn as we go on (and it is the purpose of all talking or writing on the matter to teach it) is that meditation does call us to a maturing of love and so it is a great way of purification. We are purified of our egoism and possessiveness. An ancient word that the desert fathers used to describe this process is *apatheia*. It is difficult to translate *apatheia* but it is something like 'indifference'. It is like the attitude that Job eventually had: 'The Lord gives, the Lord takes away. Blessed be the name of the Lord. If we have received good things from his hands must we not also be prepared to receive evil things?' The purpose of it all is that as we grow in fidelity, we grow in maturity and arrive at loving God

7

because of who he is. We love God as God is in himself. We love him, not because he gives us good gifts, but because he is God. We love God because he is himself: Love.

To mature at any level we have to grow through all the difficulties produced by change or loss, all the feelings, emotions and thoughts so generated and learn to love God simply and strongly. Part of the discipline of saying the mantra is that it teaches us to stay in that love, come what may. Nothing will shake us from our conviction that God is, that God is Love and that his love dwells in our hearts. If we are committed to the journey then the sense of absence will indeed deepen and strengthen our conviction of God's existence, making him more familiar, teaching us to know him more fully. At this depth of faith we are indifferent to whether we have a sense of his close presence or a sense of his absence. Whether he is near or far away in our perception or feeling does not affect the discipline that we bring to the practise of meditation because our conviction is founded not on feeling but on fact; the fact that he is the all-merciful, the all-loving, and all-compassionate God. The two silences are both of them equally powerful in teaching us: the silence of revelation fills us with wonder and the silence of absence teaches us fidelity. The Word is present in both.

> When all things began the Word already was, the Word dwelt with God, and what God was the Word was. The Word, then, was with God in the beginning and through him all things came to be, no single thing was created without him. And all that came to be was alive with his life, and that life was the light of men. The light shines on in the dark, and the darkness has never quenched it. (Jn 1:1–5)

That is the conviction we must come to in our meditation, that the darkness cannot quench the light.

8

Why we Renounce our Selves

To learn to meditate we have to learn to be profoundly silent. The way we follow is to sit absolutely, dynamically still. That is certainly the first hurdle each of us has to surmount: to learn not to fidget physically. The second thing, which is even more demanding, is to learn to say our meditation-word, the mantra, with a total attention; not to fidget mentally. Stillness and the mantra are the essentials of meditation. It is utter simplicity. Say your word and continue to say it from the beginning to the end. You will find that thoughts and distractions will appear in your mind at various levels. Don't be discouraged. The mantra helps you to plough through the distractions. Don't use any force to try to dispel them, use all your energy just saying the word.

Learning to meditate is a process, and like every process it takes time. We must learn great patience and humility. After all our education and experience it is very challenging to learn just to say our word. We have to be very patient with our slowness and with our failure to persevere. I think all of us, when we start to meditate, start and stop and start again, and all of us need courage and encouragement. The courage and the humility is to keep returning to it. The courageous and the humble are those who start again. Indeed, every time we meditate, every time we sit down to meditate we are starting again. Not surprisingly, therefore, perseverance makes us think and feel better about ourselves.

In learning to say the mantra we learn to let go of all our ideas, plans, thought-processes and, at the given moment, even of our self-consciousness. We let go of them because we know we must enter into total silence. I think it seems to all of us when we start, that the way of meditation is a negative way.

9

Silence at first seems an emptiness and an absence. Sometimes it seems extraordinarily negative. And you might well ask, 'Am I really to spend this hour like this every day – and is it necessary to meditate for a half hour in the morning and a half hour in the evening?' Other questions arise too as a result: 'Am I, in effect, turning my back on human relationships during this time? Am I being asked to abandon my own rational capacity? Am I being asked to let go of everything I've learnt? There seems so much at stake. Am I to let go of all my studies, all my professional training? Am I to abandon my own creativity?' This is what it can all seem like, at first glance. It seems that we are abandoning, one by one, each and every one of our human potentialities. For what? For stillness, for silence. For nothing. Now it is quite certain that there is no way we can come to a satisfactory answer to this sort of question, apart from the actual practice of meditation. It is only in the practice and in faith that one can find the answer but finding it does call from each of us a real leap into the dark, into the silence. It is only in the actual experience of this that we can find any satisfactory answer. This may not seem the best approach to a dialogue about meditation. But however much we can valuably say about meditation there comes a point where dialogue itself must fall silent.

I want to suggest something that may give you some reassurance as you set out on the Way. When we meditate we do indeed suspend all the separate operations of our being. But not because we reject any one of them. The mind, with all its levels of consciousness, is a wonderful gift that has been given to each of us. Our capacity for rational analysis, the power of imagination and of making distinctions, all these operations are peerless gifts given to us. Similarly, our capacity to enter into relationships with others is a priceless gift, the gift of knowing and loving another person, and of being known and of being loved. None of these gifts do we reject. But in meditation we stand back from all of them and, in that very process, we discover a harmony and an integration that become the basis of all our subsequent use of these great human gifts we have been given. The peace, the stillness and the harmony that we experience in meditation becomes the basis for all our action.

All our judgments are now illumined, inspired by love because we know that that love is the very ground of our being. Everyone who perseveres in meditation discovers that although during our time of meditation it might appear that nothing happens, yet gradually the whole of our life is changed. We have to be patient because we might like it to be changed more rapidly. Our thought gradually becomes clarified, relationships become more loving, and this is because, in the process of meditation, we are made free to love *by* Love. The reason for all this is really very simple. When we meditate, not only do we stand back from the individual operations of our being, but we begin to learn to find a wholly new ground to stand on. We discover a rootedness of being which is not just in ourselves, because we discover ourselves rooted in God. Rooted in God who is Love. All this happens because we learn the courage to take the attention off ourselves. We learn to stop thinking about ourselves and to allow ourselves to be. To be still, to be silent, is the lesson and in that stillness and silence we find ourselves in God, in love.

St Paul was writing from this rootedness to the Ephesians:

> In Christ our release is secured and our sins are forgiven through the shedding of his blood. Therein lies the richness of God's free grace lavished upon us, imparting full wisdom and insight. He has made known to us his hidden purpose – such was his will and pleasure determined beforehand in Christ – to be put into effect when the time was ripe; namely that the universe, all in heaven, all on earth, might be brought into a unity in Christ. (Eph. 1:7–10)

Meditation is the great way of unity. In the process we discover the truth of these words of St Paul for ourselves. We discover ourselves unified, made whole in Christ. Through that discovery we each find our unique and essential place in the universe, in unity with all.

The Pole

In the Letter to the Ephesians, which is one of the greatest breakthroughs of Christian revelation, St Paul describes what Jesus has achieved on behalf of the human race in extraordinarily simple terms:

> In him we have access to God with freedom, in the confidence born of trust in him. (Eph. 3:12)

Meditation in the Christian vision is also extraordinarily simple. It can in some ways be likened to climbing a hundred-foot pole. As you may know there is nothing particularly difficult about climbing a pole, once you know how to do it. It requires perseverance and at times, perhaps, you just have to hang on, get your breath and start again. To get to the top of the pole there is no alternative but to keep on climbing. As you get higher, it might happen that the view improves and then you may be tempted to stop, to give up your climbing, so that you can look at the view. I suppose that this is not entirely bad, because, after looking at the present view, you cannot help suspecting that the view will be even better at the top. But then as you keep on going up, you are quite likely to get into the clouds. And then you have no view. You have no way of knowing that you are really making any progress, except your own commitment to the climbing of one step at a time. But then the clouds clear and you discover that you were right to keep on climbing and that the view now is more magnificent than ever and you appreciate it much more having gone through the clouds.

Now that you can almost see the top of the pole, you are really encouraged to keep on climbing. But then, and this occurs very often at this stage, you begin to wonder: '*Why* am

I climbing? Can the view from the top really be that much better than here? Why not stay here? And anyway what is the purpose of the whole exercise? Is it just for a view?' But, hopefully by now, you have got used to climbing and so you decide to go on until you get to the top. And then, finally, one day, you are at the top. The view is indeed enthralling; at this stage we are usually quite pleased with ourselves. We have stayed the course, we have persevered. And then suddenly an angel of the Lord is beside us, and very quietly the angel tells us *you must jump*. You must leap. You must abandon the pole. This is the moment when we begin to understand that our faith, our commitment to Christ must be absolute if we would enter into full liberty of spirit. Everything we now are, everything we have accomplished, must be placed at his disposition. At this stage, in the face of the extraordinary insight that is given to us, many of us decide to postpone our leap, to put off our jump, our absolute commitment in faith. Postponing the moment of commitment is a terrible scourge and one that afflicts all of us, I think, to some degree. Tomorrow. Next week, next month, next year perhaps, I will take it all absolutely seriously. But for the moment I will admire the view. And I'll try to hang on as best I can. And then, *then* I will leap. But in the wonderful mercy of God the angel of the Lord comes to our aid again. The angel says to us, you must leap *now*. You must not just admire the view, you must become one with it.

The view is all creation, and the call that each and every one of us has is to take our full place within and as part of this marvellous vision of harmony, of peace, of oneness. The angel of the Lord says to us, you can't just be stuck here, on the top of this ridiculous pole. Leap. Leap into understanding, into life and into love.

Every time we meditate that is the invitation we respond to, to be on the Way, to become utterly committed to the Way. Jesus describes himself by saying, 'I am the Way'. For St Paul the Way opens to absolute fullness and infinite depth:

With this in mind, then, I kneel in prayer to the Father, from whom every family in heaven and on earth takes its name.

That out of the treasures of his glory he may grant you strength and power through his Spirit in your inner being; that through faith, Christ may dwell in your hearts in love. With deep roots and firm foundations, may you be strong to grasp, with all God's people, what is the breadth and length and height and depth of the love of Christ and to know it, though it is beyond knowledge. So may you attain to fullness of being, the fullness of God himself. (Eph. 3:14–19)

That is our leap, into the fullness of God.

Potential for 'Being'

One of the difficulties we face in learning to meditate is that it is very difficult for us to imagine that thought is not the highest and essential activity of the human being. It seems almost scandalous to a group of people who are hearing about meditation for the first time – especially if they are a religious group – when I say to them, 'You must learn not to think about God.' And if I say to them, 'Prayer is in essence not imaginatively talking to or thinking about God', the group is likely to be shocked. But it is true. We have to understand that each of us possesses a much greater potential than mere thought.

Thought is rather like sending out a signal to reality, bouncing it off reality and then interpreting the return signal. But meditation is the way wherein we become one with the reality. There is no *mediation*, there is no bouncing a signal back from reality and reading it. In meditation we are one with reality.

Now that perhaps sounds interesting, but it is just an interesting idea until you are open to the reality that is involved; unless you begin to realize your own potential for being, not just for thinking, not just for analysing or collating information, but for being. Meditation is the way of being at one with all. If we could understand our capacity for unity, for being at one with creation, with nature, with one another, then we would experience an expansion of our own potential because we would know that we are not created to be isolated. The greatest human scourge is that of loneliness. The scourge of alienation – not being able to reach others, not being able to explain yourself to them or to understand them – that is a terrible and perhaps the only ultimate tragedy. Whereas, what we are created for, each one of us, is to be at one with ourselves as the prerequisite of being at one with others. And if it is tragic

15

that we cannot understand others and others cannot understand us, it is even more tragic when we cannot understand ourselves. But such are the barriers that are to be found within us and around us. Meditation is the way of cutting through those barriers. It is the way of dismantling every barrier or ignorance, utterly and completely. Not by a process of analysis or by a process of thought, but by the process of entering utter simplicity, uncovering the simplicity of our being. If you want to put this in Christian terms you might describe meditation as the way whereby we become totally available to the gift of our own creation.

It is a way of accepting our own personhood without conditions or reservations. In that self-acceptance, and perhaps only in that way, do we become available to God. In other words, only through the experience of self-acceptance, and only this way, is it possible for us to accept God. When you begin to meditate, the less you think about God, the less you talk about God, the better. Be unconditionally open to his gift. His gift is your own personhood. No analysis is needed, no demands have to be made, only a total availability to the wonder of your own being, to the wonder of what it means to be. And the even greater wonder of what it means to be yourself, the full uniqueness of your own being. This is what the silence of meditation is about and it is to this wonder of love that silence leads you.

In Christian terms, we could describe meditation as the way of faith because it leads us through all the levels of the experience of faith. Faith in the reality of our existence. Faith in the reality of our eternal importance, the reality of our uniqueness, the reality of our present value. Imagine what it would be like if every one reading this book had some fairly adequate understanding of our human value and importance, of our wonder; and what it would be if we could communicate that understanding to only one other person. The world would be unimaginably richer by our knowing who and why we are. We would know that we are in Love and we would know it with utter certainty. Certainty is not the result of grasping a clever theological proposition but of discovering a part of ourselves, our own reality. Spiritual certainty arises from a knowledge that is not just speculative, but wholly experiential. So conditioned are we by speculative knowledge that we need to be continually reminded that in our meditation we are not involved in thinking. It is not that we despise thinking. We are not unaware of its importance. But in meditation we go beyond thinking to reality, beyond all symbols to the experience of what thought merely symbolizes.

Pure experience and faith lie along the way of simplicity. The entrance to simplicity is the door of practice. Our practice is the saying of the mantra. Say it clearly, attentively. If you can, breathe it in, and breathe out in silence. Recite it from the beginning to the end. Don't analyse it, don't analyse what you are doing. Do not think about what you are doing but be one with what you are doing. That is the first step to a oneness that you will find intoxicating, a oneness with all creation, with all beauty, a oneness with all reality, a oneness with God – which is another way of saying a oneness with Love, the basic energy of everyone and everything.

The call that each of us has unveils the potential that each of us has. It is an openness to the experience of wholly undivided consciousness, the experience of unity. All that is required is that we give this way our total attention. So for the time of the meditation, say your word, sound your word, listen to your word and abandon all else.

The mantra reflects the single-mindedness of St Paul, writing to the Galatians: 'If we are in union with Christ Jesus . . . the only thing that counts is faith, active in love' (Gal. 5:6). We say the mantra in faith and our meditation thereby becomes an activity of love.

God is the Centre of my Soul

Meditation is a very simple concept. There is nothing complicated about it, nothing esoteric. It is the simplest concept that
you could imagine and the beauty of it is that it leads us to
experience simplicity. In essence, meditation is simply being
still at the centre of your being. Being still. The only problem
connected with it is that we live in a world of almost frenetic
movement, and so stillness and rootedness seem quite foreign
to most of us. But in nature all growth is from the centre
outwards. The centre is where we begin and again that is what
meditation is about. It is making contact with the original centre
of your own being. It is a return to the ground of your being,
to your origin, to God. To know God, to grow and to be still
are all experiences at the centre of our being.

St John of the Cross, in his reflections on the nature of
meditation, wrote that 'God is the centre of my soul'. One of
the great religious dilemmas of our time is that those of us who
think of ourselves as religious are trying to understand God
with our minds, while those of us who are not overtly religious
dismiss God from our lives. What all of us have to discover is
that the only way we can talk in any meaningful way about
God is if we discover him in ourselves; if we set out on a road
of self-discovery which is the pilgrimage to our own essential
being. It is in discovering ourselves, in discovering our own
capacity for fuller being, that we find the One who is. In that
discovery we are made free and there is the great invitation of
Christianity – to discover the ground of your being and through
that discovery to experience, to encounter your own liberty.
Progress is not measured by the distance that we cover between
our origin and our destiny. Progress, in the vision of Jesus, is
simply coming to realize the vast potential we have in our

origin. All growth that endures must be thoroughly rooted and that is what meditation is for each of us, a process of becoming thoroughly rooted in the ground of our being. Meditation is a wonderful opportunity for all of us to respond to, because in returning to our origin, to the ground of our being, we return to our innocence. The call to meditation, for the early Fathers of the Church, was a call to purity of heart and that is what innocence is – purity of heart. A vision unclouded by egoism or by desire or by images, a heart simply moved by love. Meditation leads us to pure clarity – clarity of vision, clarity of understanding and clarity of love – a clarity that comes from simplicity. And to begin to meditate requires nothing more than the simple determination to begin and then to continue. *To begin* means to discover your own roots, your own potential and destiny. It is to set out on the journey both to our source and our goal.

Now let me remind you what it involves. It is the way of attention. In meditation we must go beyond thought, beyond desire and beyond imagination and in that *beyond* we begin to know that we are here and now in God, in whom 'we live, move and have our being' (Acts 17:28). The way of simplicity is the way of the one word, the recitation of the one word. It is the recitation, and the faithfulness to that recitation every morning and every evening, that leads us beyond all the din of words, beyond all the labyrinth of ideas, to oneness.

The great problems in life arise from the inability to communicate (to communicate even with ourselves) and meditation is a way into full communion, oneness of being. In meditation, and in the life enriched by meditation, we just are fully ourselves, whoever we are. That is why meditation is a school of community because in discovering our own oneness, our own being and potential, we are aware that others possess being, potential, and their unique value is what leads us to service. So, meditation is a good school of community because by it we learn both to communicate and serve. The ultimate end of meditation is communion. Not only do we discover our own oneness but we discover our oneness with *the All* and with all. The path is a path of simplicity achieved through the practice of silence. In the deep silence that each of us must discover in our own hearts, mystery is revealed and it is revealed simply because we pay attention to it.

In meditation we know because we are known. This spiritual knowledge is the basis of community and the universal Church.

> For through faith you are all children of God, in union with Christ Jesus. Baptized into union with him, you have all put on Christ as a garment. There is no such thing as Jew or Greek, slave or free man, male or female, for you are all one person in Christ Jesus. (Gal. 3:26–8)

As we meditate, we put aside all division and dividedness and we cross the divide of alienation, the divide of division, and we seek to be one with God. We find we *are* one with God.

Growth in the Presence

There are all sorts of extravagant claims made for the benefits of meditation. You can hear it said that if you work for a large organization, meditating will help you get on better with the boss. Or, it will increase efficiency and productivity, reduce stress, make you a more successful person all round. Such claims are put forward because we are so materialistic in our society that it is hard for us to realize that there can be something worth doing in and for itself, without any pay off. Why meditation is so important for us is that it helps us to realize this and to live our lives as a process of integrated growth. To live meaningfully is to know our lives as a constant, deepening maturity. Nothing I suppose is sadder than a person who lives year to year, but somehow never grows up, never truly integrates his or her experience.

Meditation is important because it leads you to that first step in all growth, which is rootedness. By meditating every morning and every evening you set out daily on the way of rootedness. Growth as a whole person unfolds by our becoming rooted in our own deepest, innermost centre. In our society all sorts of helps are given to us to grow intellectually. Not so many are given to us to grow spiritually. To find and become familiar with our spirit, the centre of our personal identity, is to begin to live from the power of that centre; no longer blown around by every wind that happens to ruffle the surface, we learn to be rooted in ourselves. Growth needs planting and rooting and it also needs cultivation. Meditation, because of its highly practical orientation, leads us day in and day out to cultivate the life of the spirit, to return to that rootedness in our centre.

Learning to sit well, still and upright is very helpful to this rooting in reality. It is the first step away from self-concern into

a whole frame of mind and of being in which we are both lost
and find ourselves in that greater reality of which we are part.

Let the mantra sound in your heart and mind, rooting you
gently in the centre. Let all peripheral thoughts and all activity
of the imagination go. Do not try to repress or erase it. Let
the constantly sounding mantra gently lead you to a depth
beyond words and thoughts and images. This is particularly
difficult for modern people because we are so used to defining
ourselves as rational creatures and unless we are engaged in
some sort of ratiocination we feel that we are not really justify-
ing our existence. Meditation can teach us simply how to *be*,
to be one, whole and attentive, in the presence of God's being.
That is what meditation is about, coming into the presence of
the One who is. And what you will discover, and you can only
discover it for yourselves, is that simply to be in his presence
is all-sufficient. That is, when you fully are the person he has
created you to be. This is not a question of pay offs or side-
benefits but of our destiny and meaning.

It is necessary to meditate every day and that too is hard for
people of our society: to undertake such a discipline that is not
concerned with what we are going to get out of it, but *simply*
concerned with being. Being the person you have been created
to be is to be rooted in your own deepest spiritual centre. The
cultivation of growth is simply the daily return, every morning
and every evening, to the practice. Saying your word, sounding
your word, and thereby entering into greater and greater simplicity. Aristotle defined eternity as a 'perpetual now'. The
power of meditating is that we seek to be fully in this present
moment, not thinking about the past, not regretting the past,
weeping over it, analysing it. Not planning for the future. God
is. God is love. God is now.

Meditation is growth *and* transcendence. Just as the plant
that is rooted and that we cultivate is in a constant state of self-
transcendence, leaving behind its former state and being what
it is now, so are we on this journey of spiritual growth. The
seed is the shoot, the shoot is the stalk, the stalk is the fruit
and so on. Meditating is just that flowing movement of self-
transcendence that unfolds as one reality – the person we are
– in God's eternal present. In meditation we are simply as

wholly and fully open to the love of this present moment as possible. If we can be faithful to it, returning every morning and every evening, our capacity for love is in a state of constant daily growth, a constant deepening of quality and expansion of range. This is what St Paul understood as the fruit of faith in the process of living the Christian life.

> So shall we all at last attain to the unity inherent in our faith and our knowledge of the Son of God – to mature manhood – measured by nothing less than the full stature of Christ. (Eph. 4:13)

Meditating is the way to unity, a total harmony between body and spirit. It is the way into the infinite mystery of God's love as we grow in a full, resonant harmony between our spirit and his spirit. Remember the way: sit still, sit upright and then, silently, deep in your heart, say your word. Say it from the beginning to the end. When you begin you will find that your thoughts stray and wander. Do not be discouraged or disheartened; you will learn to be humble. But as soon as you realize you have strayed from the word, return to it. And return to it again and again. Be faithful, be patient and find the time. Be prepared for the challenge, to meditate for a minimum of twenty minutes or for an optimum period of half an hour, every morning and every evening of your life. The journey is the journey beyond self, beyond limitation, into the limitless love of God.

Being and Existence

It is difficult for us to meditate because we are so hyper self-conscious. We cannot help, as it were, looking at the little television monitor serviced by the ego and seeing ourselves, thinking about ourselves, analysing ourselves. But meditation is concerned with a definitive silencing of that monitor screen. Meditation is a time of poverty, of silence, of self-forgetfulness, not a time for analysing ourselves, for thinking about our motives or imagining ourselves to be spiritual or sinful, but a time to be absolutely still in mind as well as body. In meditation we begin a journey and the journey is the journey to being: to be wholly open to the infinite fact that we are. There is a distinction that I think we can draw between being and existence. We can take it that being is the fact that we are, and existence is concerned with how we are. What is most important for each of us to know, to understand and to experience, is that existence flows out of being. Being is even before consciousness: remember, it is the fact that we are. Existence is all that we are familiar with, all that by which we know how we are. Being is unconditioned by anything. Existence is conditioned by everything.

In the face of the experience of death, all of us confront a hidden dread that arises out of the way we are both physically and mentally conditioned. But we cannot repress the question, 'What will it be like when we no longer know that?' So it is, that in the face of death all of us fear annihilation. And I suppose even the most developed human being cannot escape a certain anxiety in the face of annihilation. This is why our meditation is so important, to make life courageous about death.

Meditation is the journey beyond our existence to our being.

To our own unique being. It is the journey to the essential core of what and who we are. The wonderful thing we know in the Christian revelation is that, even more than that, it is the journey into the heart of Being itself. It is the journey into God. The One who made us *who* we are. For everyone of us it is of supreme importance that we do travel beyond the existential dread, because we must travel beyond fear. Fear paralyzes, fear reduces us to an inhuman state, whereas love sets us free. We must set out on this journey for ourselves if we are to see, in the light of the Christian gospel, that the journey is beyond ourselves into absolute and essential being. Being who is God, the God who is Love. Living and dying is the destiny of each one of us. We must live well but we must die well too. We can only do either if we learn to live from the root of our being and if we learn and integrate the knowledge in our own experience, that each of us has our being rooted in eternal Being, in God.

Now, all that is a jungle of words. What is of supreme importance to each of us is that we *know* it. We must know it with the knowledge that arises directly from our own being, beyond consciousness, beyond all ratiocination. It is not the knowledge of books or even of speech. It is the knowledge that language only imperfectly communicates because language itself is a child of this knowledge. It is pure experience, knowledge that is rooted not only in the bedrock of our own being but beyond our own being, in God. The way to it is a very simple way. It is the way of silence, the way of faithfulness, the way of poverty of spirit. A generous poverty is a joyful one in which we surrender all our thoughts, all our imagination, all our words and stay with the one word, the mantra. When you begin you have to take this on faith; you have to say your word beyond all reason. And then you have to come back to your meditation every morning and every evening. You have to give up the categories that we are conditioned to using of success or failure, whether it is working or not working and to go on simply, in childlike faith, to say your mantra. Say your word. The wonderful power of it is that the very exercise of this childlike faith brings us back to our innocence and the freedom of innocence. We learn to be in the presence of Being. Simple, still, loving and utterly free: in meditation and in daily life, in mind and body.

I have been crucified with Christ. The life I now live is not my life, but the life which Christ lives in me, and my present bodily life is lived by faith in the Son of God, who loved me and who sacrificed himself for me. (Gal. 2:20)

That is the experience of Christian meditation, living our lives out of the root power of God. The power is revealed to us, in our own hearts, in the risen person of Jesus.

'Isness'

More and more people are aware that somehow or other, in modern life, we have lost contact with what is essential. Contact is lost with our own essential being, our own centre. The problem we face, as a consequence, is that we have ceased to look upon our religious practice or our spiritual practice in terms of a discipline. More often we look upon our religious or spiritual commitment in terms of what we get out of it. We had a young man from London staying with us last year and as we were talking one day he said something to this effect: 'You know, Father John, you'll be shocked when you hear this, but I gave up religion because I wasn't getting anything out of it. Blimey, when I think of it now I wake up in the night and cold shivers run down my spine. Imagine, *I* was thinking what *I* was going to get out of it.' He had begun to remake contact.

I imagine all of us have adopted this ego-centred approach to our religious or spiritual practice at some time. We too need to examine the true nature of our religious life to find a way to begin decreasing the egotistical element in it. We need to be grasped by the truth that religious values are not to be exploited or experimented with because they – and the sacred they represent – call on us for commitment. As soon as we have begun to commit ourselves we have begun a journey. It is a journey that asks for discipline, and the challenge to us is that it is a journey away from our own egoism. Many of us even start to meditate because we have need of an attractive image of ourselves as wise, enlightened, spiritually powerful. Others want tricks and go about getting bumps on their head from hitting the ceiling. There are many motives. But we have to learn that meditation is a journey away from all self-coloured motives, that is, away from all images of ourselves. It is a

27

journey into reality and starting to meditate is undertaking the lifelong commitment to become, and to be yourself.

And so, meditation is not about making something happen. What it is about, and this is the basic aim of meditation, is to become fully aware of, fully inserted into, fully grounded in *what is*. If we wanted to invent a term to describe something that precedes all language we could say that meditation is about *isness*. You remember how in Exodus God describes himself simply in the words, '*I am* . . . tell them, *I am* sent you.' *I am* is the present tense of the verb to be and God is, essentially, *present being*. Meditation is full openness to our own present being. What you can learn from meditating is that your being comes to fullness when you are wholly open to the one who is *I am*.

Isness is the experience of God that completes and renews us and it is quite inaccessible for anyone who has not learned to be simple. Learning to meditate is learning this. Meditation leads us to the threshold over which only God's grace can then lead us. My advice to you is to read as few books as possible about meditation. The important factor is the practice. The tradition that we speak from is eminently practical when it teaches the importance of still and quiet sitting. Always take a few moments to find a comfortable sitting posture and learn to relax your body as you prepare to meditate. Do not consciously practise any body-postures or exercises during the meditation, but you may well find that some attention to how you prepare will help you.

The essential rule of posture is to hold your spine upright. In addition I recommend you to close your eyes lightly and breathe regularly. It is a very important part of the discipline to learn to sit absolutely still. You will feel like moving or scratching your nose or opening your eyes but in sitting still you are taking a very important lesson in this journey away from egoism, away from self-obsession. Simply sitting still for a fixed period of time is also a real experience of the transcendence of desire. And so, sitting as still as you can, begin to say your word. The essence of meditating is learning to recite – from the beginning until the end of your meditation – a word that is called in some traditions, a mantra. And the essential teaching of meditation is contained in this short phrase: *say your mantra.*

It is almost impossible for people starting to believe there could be anything very significant in sitting still, closing your eyes lightly and just reciting a word. You have to take that on faith when you begin and it is also helpful to be given your word. The word I recommend you to repeat is the Aramaic word *maranatha.* It means 'Come, Lord'. But do not bother about thinking what it means, and it is not necessary to start looking around for other or 'better' words. In addition, do not think about God. In fact do not think about anything. Say your word, recite it and listen to it.

I first started to meditate like this about thirty years ago. I suppose that I was as crass as anyone of my age because I was always saying to the man who taught me: 'How long is this going to take? I can't sit around here saying this word forever, you know.' He would look at me with a rather pained look, and either he would just look straight through me or else he would say, 'Say your mantra.' Thirty years later I am still astonished at the wisdom of that teaching. As I say, you have to take it on faith when you begin. Nothing that I can say or, I suppose, that anyone can say will be very significant for you in comparison with the persuasive power of your own experience. You will enter into profounder and profounder silence. You will enter into clearer and clearer simplicity. The author of *The Cloud of Unknowing,* who teaches this doctrine from fourteenth-century England, said that very often he gets objections to his teaching from learned people and from theologians. But, he said, rarely do objections come from simple people. The most frequent objections are that this is a complex, esoteric doctrine. But it is not. It is a doctrine of utter simplicity. It requires no more than faith. It requires the sort of faith that you need to leap into a clear blue lake. Someone who has gone in before you says, 'Come on, it's not cold' (maybe looking very blue as they say so). You just have to have the faith to plunge in. And that is the sort of faith you require to say your mantra. To say the mantra is to cease being an observer on the sidelines weighing up your chances of success.

The only other thing you need to know is that it is essential to say your mantra every day of your life, every morning and every evening. This again is difficult to understand because we have so little understanding of spiritual discipline. But we *need* to put aside about half an hour every morning and half an hour every evening, to be still, to be simple and, in the language of the very early monastic fathers, to rest in the Lord. An honoured word they used to describe their meditation was *quies*, rest, being quiet, being still. At that moment of *quies* you are not concerned about what you will do; you are wholly concerned about being. If everyone in this room could *be* the person they are called to be, then all their doing would be right. Whatever we did would be right. This is the problem that each of us faces personally and our society faces collectively. It is a communal task for us to learn again how to live properly, fully, humanly. Meditation will teach you that living fully means expanding, crossing the frontiers of your own limitations. Crossing the frontier of your own being you find yourself in God. So do not think that stillness is static or that *quies* is passive. In peace we find the God who conceives and sustains a cosmos.

Remember, meditation is not about making something happen – you or the cosmos. It has all happened. Each day everyone of us has the potential within ourselves along with the means, to become fully the person we are called to be. That potential and the means is nothing less than the presence of Jesus Christ in our hearts. Meditation is simply being open to that.

You might find it helpful at times, especially when you meditate in a group with others, to prepare for the meditation period with some suitable music, the purpose of which is to forget all the preceding words, to forget the ideas, to empty your mind of anxious concerns. It can prepare you gently to say your word gently. You should say your word with the simplicity of a child. Do not ask yourself, 'What am I getting out of this? Is this philosophically sound?' Put all those questions aside at the time. Say the mantra from the depth of your being, in all simplicity. For the rest, if we can make ourselves available, if we can be there, everything else is given. Everything is gift beyond that. What is necessary for us is to be there. And meditation is the simple way of being there. We are realizing the new era which Jesus has inaugurated:

His divine power has bestowed on us everything that makes for life and true religion, enabling us to know the One who called us by his own splendour and light. And through this might and splendour he has given us his promises, great beyond all price, and through them you may escape the corruption with which lust has infected the world, and you may come to share in the very being of God. (2 Pet. 1:3–4)

This is the spiritual reality within which we have our being: *sharing in the very being of God.* The way to realize this reality is the way of discipline and seriousness of purpose, of daily return to the discipline. It is the way of simplicity, of fidelity and, as you will find, it is the way of love.

The Barrier of Distractions

I am sure you have reflected on what it is that brings each of us to meditate. People must have a pretty strong desire to meditate to come out to talks on meditation on cold winter nights and then to undertake a new spiritual discipline that they, with difficulty, begin to incorporate into their already overcrowded lives. I think it is that some instinct in us tells us that we must go deeper. We can never be content just to live at the usual surface level of activities and distractions. Some spiritual instinct tells us that there is a great wealth and a great power to be found if only we can learn to be still and mindful. The great interest in meditation in our society is symptomatic of the self-evident limitations of material things to bestow any ultimate satisfaction or meaning. More and more people in our busy, shallow society are discovering that they must find how to live their lives at a deeper and at a richer level. We are beginning to understand how urgent it is that we do not allow ourselves to be trivialized. We must refuse to be conditioned to be content to live at the surface. We must insist on the need to make contact with the depth of our being.

One of the first things we discover as we start to meditate is that we are already chock full of distractions and that it is not so easy to go beyond that surface level of distracted planning and analysis, to the depth. It is very humbling, not to say humiliating, to discover that after all our education with all the credits we have clocked up in so many clever areas of expertise, we cannot be still for more than a few moments and that our mind wanders off on the most ridiculous sidetracks. It ambles on, creating the most ridiculous fantasies with thoughts flying around at every level in our mind. We cannot be still. When you begin, and as you make that humbling discovery, you will

32

soon face two temptations. The first is to give up completely and say, 'This is hopeless, it is not worth it, it is all beyond me.' The second temptation is to say 'Let me analyse what is happening.' The first temptation is to despair, or to evade the challenge. The second is the temptation to self-obsession, to become immoderately interested and engaged by your own mental processes.

Now the art of meditation is to teach you the discipline to continue, and to continue on a daily basis, as one who is committed to depth, to seriousness, to fullness of life. That is, to be one who rejects living at the surface as one's normal and necessary state of being. Meditation will gradually increase your discipline and your commitment will grow proportionately if you stick to it as a daily practice. Meditation will also teach you to turn away from your self, to rise above your own thoughts, to be detached from your own self-consciousness, vanities, fears and desires. It will lead you to turn naturally beyond that to something much greater than you can ever find in all the analysis or self-obsession our culture rates so highly. You have begun a journey through the undergrowth of the ego and the way through is the way of the mantra. You need to know only a few things to meditate. You must be still and in the first few weeks learn to *sit* absolutely still as the first step in *being* absolutely still. Then start to say your mantra ceaselessly, continually. The mantra builds up the power in you to keep going, and it is the mantra above all that takes your attention off yourself, that cuts through self-consciousness. It seems as though when you start to meditate you are caught in an endless storm of distraction. There are flashes of lightning going on all around and there are howling gales blowing in all directions. The mantra is like a beacon guiding us through and we must keep our attention on it. If we take our attention off the mantra we are lost. We return again to self-consciousness, to self-obsession, to confusion. It is *extraordinarily* simple.

What does this mean in Christian terms? It means, simply, that there is only the prayer of Jesus. His is the one prayer and that prayer is the stream of his consciousness fully open to the Father. The wholly extraordinary truth about the Christian proclamation is that each one of us, wherever we start from, is invited to open our consciousness fully to the consciousness of Jesus, and, in that openness, to be taken out of ourselves, beyond ourselves, into that stream of conscious love which flows between Jesus and the Father. That is the personal destiny of each one of us and in that experience we are made completely and eternally real. The paradox is to know yourself for the first time because you are lost in God. That is what the gospel tells us, 'Whoever would find his life must lose it.' Meditation is a sure way of losing your own life, losing your own consciousness of yourself as an autonomously separate, separated entity. In losing it you find yourself at one with God and at one with all creation because you are now at last one with yourself. Your consciousness is no longer divided, no longer confused. It is simplified. It is one in God.

Remember therefore the simplicity of meditation. My recommendation to you when you are beginning (the first five years) is to read as few books as possible on the subject. Talk about it as little as possible. Think about it as little as possible. But meditate every day and when you have been meditating for a few years then, if you have the inclination to do so, you can read some books. Then you can perhaps talk usefully about it. Our society is much given to studying things in as much detail and variety as possible, but in meditation the invitation is not to study. It is to enter in, to taste, to see and to know how good God is. To taste and to see and to know how good *you* are in him.

The discipline of meditation will lead you to a liberty that intoxicates with the joy and peace of the Spirit and sets all your life-experience in the supremely Christian framework of hope:

> May the God of hope fill you with all joy and peace by your faith in him until by the power of the Holy Spirit you overflow with hope. (Rom. 15:13)

Here is the Christian invitation, therefore, no longer to live at the surface, not to live at the level of glitter and triviality, but to be filled with the peace and with the love of God. In the fullness that ensues you discover your own full reality; discover yourself made real in God.

Returning to Innocence

One of the greatest forces that resists life is fear and fear is largely the fear of being punished or of dying. Fear, death, life and love are the actors in the Christian drama.

> In very truth, anyone who gives heed to what I say and puts his trust in him who sent me has hold of eternal life and does not come up for judgment but has already passed from death to life. (Jn 5:24)

That is the truth of the gospel that each of us is invited not just to read, but to live. The gospel of Jesus is about living. It is about life and all of us are invited to live our lives not, as it were, at fifty or sixty percent of our potential, but at a hundred percent: to live life with fullness. The witness of the gospel proclaims that this is only possible for any of us if we are fully in touch with our life-source, which is the source of all life, the Divine energy. Jesus spoke to 'anyone who gives heed to what I say'. We have to learn to *listen* to him, to listen deeply to the invitation to live our lives to the full and so to be filled with divine power. We have to listen with the fullness of our own being, profoundly, totally. That is why the silence of meditation is so important and why each of us, through our own experience as we continue to meditate, discovers that silence is so precious a value in our lives in general. Silence also touches our common life together so that we can share a sense of the mysterious power both in our midst and beyond us.

'And puts his trust in him who sent me.' Meditation is a way of returning to our own innocence and so of learning to trust as a child; as we used to trust before the experience of betrayal, before we ourselves had become betrayers. But the great message of hope of the gospel is that because our sins are forgiven, our betrayals are forgiven and we can return to that early fullness of life, through fullness of trust, wholly innocent and wholly loving. To love in innocence is to be wholly trusting. In meditation this is what we know, that we live from this power. We know that we are forgiven, we know the wonder of the difference that has been made for each of us by the life, death and resurrection of Jesus. Each of us is invited to know this uniquely, for ourselves, and so to respond fully to the gift of our own life. Innocence is characterized by trust and Jesus says that we must trust the Father, 'putting his trust in him who sent me'. It is the fundamental challenge and invitation to the Christian because to trust we have to let go. To trust we have to come to rest in him and to allow ourselves to be held by him. Meditation opens up the experience, to which each of us is called, of the interior reality of the theological virtues, the reality of faith, the reality of hope, the reality of love: a triune reality realized by the innocent act of trust.

Through meditation we come to know those inter-connected realities fully, in the depth of our being. I think we could say that meditation is the activity of total peace in an all-encompassing silence. In the silence of meditation we love all, we love *the* All. The way is the way of discipline, the way of stillness and silence, the way of the mantra. We do not seek anything except total truth, total love because we know that we can only find fullness in God. Finding it, we are ourselves enlivened with his life and enlightened with his light. Jesus assures us that if we will listen and if we will trust we will not come up for judgment: 'He who puts his trust in him who sent me has hold of eternal life and does not come up for judgment but has already passed from death to life.' This is because in that act of trust we cannot but choose God when we know ourselves chosen by him: that is the passing from death to life and Jesus tells us, 'The Father has in him life-giving power and so has the Son by the Father's gift.'

It is a remarkable thing that all of us who read these words should have been given the gift of knowing that there is this life-giving power, in the Father's gift freely given; *lavished upon us*, as St Paul says. None of us could have merited that knowledge and yet it is given to us. One thing is necessary and that is that we respond to it and because the gift is total, the response must be total. That is the active totality of the mantra: nothing else, no thoughts, no words, no imagination, just the mantra. And why? So that we may be totally available to that gift and to its Giver. When we are starting, the discipline seems hard; it sometimes seems too demanding. But the discipline is nothing compared to the gift. I want to encourage every one of you to listen to these words of Jesus and to know that they are addressed to you. Your invitation is to come to fullness of knowledge, fullness of life and fullness of love, and we must not settle for anything less. The gift is too great and the Giver too lovable for less than a total response.

> In truth, in very truth, I tell you, a time is coming, indeed it is already here, when the dead shall hear the voice of the Son of God and all who hear shall come to life. For as the Father has life-giving power in himself, so has the Son by the Father's gift. (Jn 5:25–6)

Let us be open to that life-giving power.

The Listening Heart

This is a scene from the life of Jesus in the Gospel of St Luke:

> They even brought babies for him to touch, but when the disciples saw them they scolded them for it. But Jesus called for the children and said, 'Let the little ones come to me. Do not try to stop them. For the Kingdom of God belongs to such as these. I tell you that whoever does not accept the Kingdom of God like a child will never enter it.' (Lk. 18:15–17)

Learning to meditate is learning to unlearn. The big problem that faces anyone who starts to meditate is the simplicity of it. God is One. And Christian prayer has been described as the way of one-ing, becoming one, becoming one with the One who is One. The problem we face is to leave complexity behind. We are used to complexity because we are brought up to believe that the more perfect the technique, the more stunning will be the result. The perfecting of techniques increases complexity. The perfecting of a discipline leads to simplicity. And Jesus tells us to become simple, to become childlike. Meditation is the way of rediscovering our innate, childlike sense of wonder. Christian prayer is a state of innocence. When we meditate we go beyond desire, beyond possessiveness, beyond self-importance, beyond all sources of guilt and complexity. So the first thing you must learn when you set out on the pilgrimage of meditation is to listen to the message with the simplicity of a child. God is One. And the extraordinary thing about the Christian proclamation is that our vocation is to be one with him, in him and through him.

To meditate you must learn to be still. Meditation is perfect stillness of body and spirit. In that stillness we open our hearts to the eternal silence of God, to be swept out of ourselves, beyond ourselves, by the power of that silence. So the first thing to learn is to sit completely still and the only essential rule of posture is that your spine is as upright as possible. Take a couple of moments at the beginning of each meditation to sit still; get a comfortable posture and sit as upright as you can. Your eyes should be lightly closed. And then interiorly, silently, in your heart, begin to say your word, your mantra. The word I recommend is *maranatha*. And that is all you have to do. Don't think about God, don't work up in yourself any holy feelings about God. Christian meditation is far more than thinking or feeling about God. It is being with him, living not just in his presence but from the resources of his presence. We are able to live with his power, while being united to his power and his power is the basic energy of all creation, the power of love. That power is a mighty river flowing in and through our hearts and in meditating what we do is to open our hearts to the pure reality of that stream of love. Where are we when we meditate? We are in God. Where is God? He is in us. Quite simply, this is the great conviction of the early Church, of all Christ's disciples. The presence in our heart is that of the living Christ, and the supreme task of every life that would be fully human is to be open to that presence.

The message that we have for the world is one that we cannot communicate unless we know it ourselves. The message we have to pass on is that we each have, within us, all the elements that make for wisdom, for understanding, for kindness, for gentleness, for compassion. Everything we need to be able to meet others is there, to be found and enjoyed in our own hearts.

The word of hope that we have to communicate to the world is that what mankind needs is not possessiveness but thankfulness, not desire but enjoyment, not self-importance but love. To come to this wisdom we need to learn to be silent, to be humble, and this we learn by being attentive to the presence in our hearts. To learn to meditate it is necessary to meditate every day: every morning and every evening. Learning is a discipline and we have to be generous with our time, with our energy, with our attention. We have to be generous. We can

never learn to enter into the supreme self-giving generous love
of God without that generous commitment to the Way and to
the discipline of the Way.

It is not good enough to talk or read about religion or spirituality. It is not good enough to study or have a spiritual director.
We must enter personally into the basic Christian experience
and we can only do so with childlike simplicity. This connection
between simplicity and discipline explains why it is important
to say your word from the beginning to the end. All of us
have such an appalling hunger for self-analysis, for self-
preoccupation which often masquerades as spirituality, that if
we used the time of meditation to satisfy this desire it would
be entirely counter-productive. We would fail to meet our
deepest need which is for unity. The essence of meditation is
taking the attention off ourselves and looking forward, beyond
ourselves, into the mystery of God; of travelling beyond ourselves into his love, into union.

So let me stress to you the importance of saying the word.
Do not think about God, do not think about yourself. Do not
analyse God, do not analyse yourself. Be silent. Be still and
be with him, in his presence.

Reciprocal indwelling is one of the great themes of St John
in his Gospel and first letter,

> You therefore must keep in your heart that which you heard
> at the beginning. If what you heard then still dwells with
> you, you will yourselves dwell in the Son and also in the
> Father and this is the promise that he himself gave us: the
> promise of eternal life. (1 Jn 2:24–5)

That promise holds today and each time we meditate. Eternal
life means limitless life and what everyone of us must know
from our own experience is that that limitless life of God is to
be found in our own hearts. St John goes on, 'Even now, my
children, dwell in him, so that when he appears we may be
confident and unashamed before him, at his coming.'

We can be sure that he dwells within us because we know it
from the Spirit he has given us. The way of meditation is a way
of sureness because it enjoys the utter simplicity of the spirit
of unity.

Beyond All Images

One of the questions that we often discuss at the groups meeting at the Priory is about the view we are to take concerning the progress we make in meditation. It is a natural question to arise in the minds of people who live in our sort of society because we are conditioned to think in terms of progress: that we are getting somewhere, that we are achieving something. Yet as you will know if you have been meditating for sometime, progress is not really a thing, a quality or quantity, that you can very usefully consider. Meditation is a way of coming to an immeasurable reality beyond all images. The problem we face on this journey is that we have to sidestep our own ego which is the supreme manufacturer of images, mostly images of ourselves and, to a lesser extent, images of others, even images of God.

When you begin to meditate, the ego is immediately reactive. It regroups its threatened forces and proposes to you the question, 'Are you wasting your time at this? What progress are you making? Where are you getting?' If you have a rather stubborn sort of nature and continue to meditate in spite of taunts like these, your ego will probably try another tack. It will say, 'You are doing tremendously well, you are going to be a saint, you are a born mystic. This is marvellous. How many other people can have the capacity for such silence as you have?' And so the ego begins to manufacture for you the image of the truly spiritual man or woman. Before long that image is fractured and you are back where you started. There are countless ways the ego will try to discourage you, to stop you meditating, because the ego knows right from the beginning that if you meditate, if you *do* go beyond all image to the reality, then the ego is finished. It will be dethroned. It will lose power.

Now think for a moment of your own experience of meditation. You know that you begin, you seem to make progress and then you fail. For most of us, all our experience of meditation is contained in starting and stopping, in getting somewhere and finding that we are nowhere, in elation and discouragement. What you have to learn from this experience is that you must simply say your mantra. It is perfectly natural for you to pose the question, 'What good is this doing for me? What progress am I making?' but it is also perfectly useless. Indeed, it is worse than perfectly useless, it is positively counterproductive.

Now, why should you meditate therefore? I think all of us answer that question eventually in this way: at various times in our lives, all of us have wanted to be committed to truth, to be committed to God. Meditation answers that need. I was talking to a group of priests recently and it was their common experience that sometime at the beginning of their lives, and later in the seminary, they all wanted to serve God. They wanted to serve him firstly by being wholly open and generous to him in their prayer, and then they tried to pray and got nowhere. They then became discouraged but when they voiced their discouragement, the counsel they received was, 'You are going to be priests with an active life. Do the best you can in your prayers. Say your prayers and leave real praying to the experts.' Now what we know, I think, is that all of us have tried, all of us have wanted to pray and all of us have failed. But at some time we come to the conclusion that the wisdom we receive from the contemplative tradition of prayer is *the* wisdom that turns the failure into triumph. The silence and poverty we experience in our meditation become self-authenticating. We know that we cannot analyse God. We know that we cannot, with finite minds, understand the infinitude of God. But we also know, or at least we soon begin dimly to suspect, that we can experience God's love for us. Knowing that set us on a road that somehow strikes us as authentic and it is this knowledge that keeps us going. It is this experiential knowledge that teaches us, too, that the images manufactured by the ego, whether of hopelessness or of sanctity, must all give way. None of them can be taken seriously. Every new strategy of the ego has to be laughed at and dismissed.

Success and failure give way to what we come to know to be true through our own experience of meditation: death and resurrection. Every time we sit down to meditate we die to self and we rise beyond our own limitations to new life in Christ. We know that it is his life within us, his indwelling Spirit in our hearts, which is real and the essential energy of our *growth*. We also know that we can only come to our full potential if we are rooted in that reality, rooted in that love and living out of its power. We have to learn to say our mantra. We have to learn to say it from the beginning of our meditation until the end. We have to understand that it is the daily discipline of our meditation that finally unmasks the ego. Unmasked, it disappears. We must not be impatient or despondent. We must say our mantra, with faith, day after day. Success or failure will then have no significance. The only thing that is significant is the reality of God, the reality of his presence in our heart, and our own reality as we respond to that presence. The discipline we first of all learn from our physical stillness. This is why we have to learn to sit still throughout our meditation, and then we learn the discipline from the faithful repetition of our mantra.

The Christian life means living in Christ and living out of his power. Consider how St Paul described it in the Letter to the Philippians:

> I count everything sheer loss because all is far outweighed by the gain of knowing Christ Jesus my Lord, for whose sake I did in fact lose everything and I count it as so much garbage for the sake of gaining Christ and finding myself incorporate in him. . . . All I care for is to know Christ and to experience the power of his resurrection. (Phil. 3:8–9, 10)

That is what meditation is about – in the silence and poverty of your meditation to know Christ, and to experience in your own heart the power of his resurrection.

From Isolation to Love

This is a word of hope from the Letter to the Ephesians:

> Your world was a world without hope and without God but now in union with Christ Jesus you who once were far off have been brought near through the shedding of Christ's blood, for he himself is our peace. (Eph. 2:12–13)

When you have been meditating long enough, you come to know that a person meditates because it is the natural and indeed the obvious thing to do. We meditate because we know with absolute certainty that we must pass through and beyond our own sterility. We must transcend the sterility of the closed system, of a purely introspective mind. We know, with an ever greater clarity, that we have to pass beyond isolation into love. It is curious that introspection, the mind turned in upon itself, should lead to such sterility. Why should a self-centred consciousness be so sterile? Suppose for example we try to analyse some experience of our own. The almost inevitable consequence is that we end up observing ourselves in the act of analysis and we end up in the state of analysing our self-observation. The deeper the degree to which we turn in upon ourselves, the more complex will be the degree to which we become fixated upon our own self-consciousness. The result is like being trapped in a hall of mirrors where we constantly take the image for reality. And all we have are images of ourselves.

This is a good point to ask why is meditation so different? I think it is true to say that all of us begin meditating as egoists and the first crisis we come to is when in our meditation itself we experience egoism's sterility, dryness, nothingness. All of us, I think, when we begin, come to a point when we ask ourselves 'What am I getting out of this? What is it doing for me?' or, 'Is this the same as everything else? Am I going to end up here, too, with nothing but sterility?' The temptation, of course, is to give up, to fly from this new and perhaps even deeper sterility. It is at this point that all of us have to make an act of faith. It may appear to be the faith to enter the darkness and to embrace the sterility, but there is no way we can embrace it except with total abandon. It has to be a total act of faith. In other words, we commit ourselves to meditation, and to the mantra as a way to commit ourselves, to letting go of self-consciousness. In effect, we are committing ourselves to letting go of our own sterility.

It is at this point that the sterility we experience is transformed into poverty – a poverty that we embrace totally. Here we are led to that declaration of our own poverty which reveals that there is only God and in God are all riches and all love. This is what made St Francis such a great religious genius. He knew and experienced this commitment to total poverty. Commitment to poverty is what makes meditation such a strange process. It takes time for our conscious mind to keep abreast with what is happening in our deepest being. We are slow to understand the transformation that is taking place. That is why it is so important simply to continue, to continue meditating day after day, morning and evening, and to continue saying the mantra, without trying to analyse our progress. Our progress is in God and we cannot analyse God or even our experience of God.

Sterility becomes poverty. Poverty is a state of complete simplicity, complete vulnerability and complete abandon to God and to his love. Self-consciousness gives way to consciousness. We become aware of what is beyond our own horizons, of what *is*, what God is: that God is Love. Introspection is transformed into self-transcendent vision because everything we see, we now see in the divine light, expanded into infinity. We see everything bathed in the infinite love of God. We must understand very clearly why this is so. It is because we ourselves are committed to the Way by means of fidelity to meditation and the mantra: commitment to God. Commitment is faith. Faith is commitment to what is beyond us and in this way we take possession of our destiny to find our meaning in the wonder of God. That is why it is so supremely important that each of us is utterly serious about our commitment to joy, to love and to God, which we find on the journey.

What you will know from your own experience is that there are no half-measures. We cannot be half-committed. Just as in meditation itself, its absolute simplicity is that we either say the mantra or we do not. We cannot half say it. And so let me urge you to commit yourselves, or perhaps better, allow yourselves to be committed, to say your mantra, to enter in upon your inheritance. The inheritance that is yours in Christ. That inheritance is no less than to know absolute liberty of spirit in union, in union with God.

This is how Paul continues his teaching of hope to the Ephesians:

> This is in accord with his age-long purpose which he achieved in Christ Jesus our Lord. In him we have access to God with freedom, in the confidence born of trust in him. (Eph. 3:11–12)

In our meditation as we say our mantra, let us do so in absolute trust in him.

A Meaningful Life

One of the influences of modern life we are all subject to is that of advertising. Modern advertising is inevitably concerned with what is new, with proclaiming novelty, and so in much of our experience of life, of reality, we are conditioned to be nervously concerned about what is new, what is the latest. The result is that instead of seeing life as a whole and as a process of growth, of maturity and of integrating depth and surface levels, we merely move from one thing to another. We easily lose the sense of connectedness between events and our lives can drift imperceptibly into a state of being continually distracted. Novelties are the distractions; one following the other, with the thinnest thread of association, or even none at all. As most people are discovering today, if we do live our lives just moving from one novelty to another, we very quickly find a frightening sort of dullness setting in. For nothing seems to satisfy us if we are only concerned with things that are outside of ourselves.

Now the way of meditation is a serious attempt to live life and to understand life no longer in terms of always finding some novelty. We seek an understanding infinitely greater than that. We are led to an understanding that life, each and every moment of it, is perpetually new. This newness is not just a passing novelty, because you discover that in every moment you are springing from the creative hand of God. Godlike newness underpins all life as ultimate reality. Human novelty is the most fragile of life's superstructures. If you can learn to start living from the depths of this underpinning reality, which are also the depths of your own being, you will encounter your own capacity, your own potential. You will then soon discover that life is always marvellously fresh, continually exciting

47

because it is always expanding. Your sights are always stretching forward into infinity, not contracting into this or that passing object of satisfaction. This is why a person meditates.

We meditate because we understand that the human spirit was created precisely for an infinite expansion of being. But we must always be careful not to be misled by the intoxication of language. The way forward is on to a journey which is truly adventurous, leading you into the infinite depths and ultimately to infinite expansion, because your heart, your entire being, is created for union with the infinite God. It is an adventure but it is a journey that demands discipline. We would be very foolish only to dream about the vision and fail actually to take the steps required to enter the vision. Do not be misled by the idea of discipline. Everyone is invited to tread this path. Discipline is a universal norm. The whole thrust of the New Testament and of the ensuing Christian revelation is that every man and woman alive has been brought into being for this very growth, for depth, maturity and union with God. Now what must we do? How do we set out on this adventure of our own creation?

If you want to meditate, the first thing you require is to be serious about it. Not solemn. But serious. To see this as a serious invitation will lead you to the deepest personal actualization of your potential. If you want to learn to meditate, you must put aside the time for it every day of your life. Ideally you should find a time every morning and every evening. The morning time of meditation sets the tone for the day and prepares you to set out on your daily pilgrimage knowing better who you are. Then your evening meditation brings together all the various strands of the day's activities, and unifies them through your own concentration. So you must understand that the daily discipline is of immense importance. You cannot make the journey by just admiring the spiritual realities from a distance. You must enter. You must taste and see. The time I recommend you to spend in meditation is a minimum of twenty minutes and an optimum time of half an hour, every morning and every evening.

Meditating is in itself utterly simple. You take your word, your mantra – the word I recommend you to take is *maranatha*, and you say it by articulating the four syllables. Give equal strength to each one: *ma – ra – na – tha*. Find your own rhythm for saying it and then recite the word in silence, in the depths of your spirit. Do not analyse. Do not ask yourself, 'Am I enjoying this?' Do not ask yourself, 'Am I getting anything out of this?' Let the self-reflective consciousness switch off and just say the word, in your heart, continuously, from the beginning to the end. Do not think, do not imagine, do not entertain any words that come into your consciousness but just say your mantra from beginning to end. Sit as still as you can, as silently as you can. Meditating is that wonderful state of total harmony between body and spirit in the absolute unity of perfect silence. And so, when you meditate prepare with a few moments to get really comfortable. The only essential rule of posture is that your spine is kept upright, as upright as you can comfortably make it. Sit straight. Then sit still throughout your meditation. Do not move, as movement will be a distraction. That outward stillness is no small discipline but it is a great sign of the inward stillness that will come as you say your mantra.

The purpose of meditating is to advance along the way of the fullness of your own humanity. Meditating is simply accepting the gift of our creation and developing the potential we have to respond to the gift fully. We are not people who have to live on the surface, or people who are condemned to live lives of shallow emotion. Meditating is leaving the shallows, leaving the surface and entering into the depths of your own being. The reason why, in the Christian tradition, we meditate, is that we believe that Jesus has sent his Spirit into these depths to dwell in our heart. Or, to use other words, the Spirit of God, the Spirit of the Creator of the universe dwells in our hearts and in silence is loving to all. In the Christian tradition, meditating is simply being open to the Spirit of Love, the Spirit of God.

The fulfillment of human nature is at the centre of Christian teaching. It is what St Paul was asserting in his words to the Colossians:

Therefore since Jesus was delivered to you as Christ and Lord, live your lives in union with him. Be rooted in him;

be built in him. . . . For it is in Christ that the complete being of the Godhead dwells embodied. And in him you have been brought to completion. (Col. 2:6–7, 9)

The essential message of Christianity is that our call and our potential is to enter into the life of God through Jesus, through his Spirit present in our heart. We do this, not by analysing God or analysing Jesus, not by thinking about God or thinking about Jesus, but by being silent and still and, in his Spirit's presence, opening our hearts to his love. We do so in the steady rhythm of our daily meditation. There is a great paradox to face. People looking at meditation from the outside see it as dull repetition. They see the saying of the mantra as something so repetitive as to be almost impossible. But if you really learn to say the mantra, that is, if you really learn to meditate, you will find that the mantra can never become mere repetition. It never becomes boring, because it is always, in new depths, taking you beyond yourself. It is always opening your spirit to what is beyond, to more of the infinity of God.

But these are only words. You can only learn this from your own experience. And you can learn it, if only you can learn to say your mantra, not thinking about yourself, not surveying yourself in the silence of meditation but by letting go of thought and all self-concern. Say the word with the simplicity of a child. As St Paul says elsewhere, the secret of life is Christ because in Christ lie hidden all the treasures of God's wisdom and knowledge. The astonishing thing is that Christ himself is to be found in our own hearts. Learning to say your mantra is simply setting out on this pilgrimage to your own heart, there to find all the treasures of wisdom and knowledge.

Freedom in Being

Something that everybody is interested in today and that has profoundly affected the consciousness of people of our time is the question of freedom. Everybody wants to be free. But there are various ways of understanding freedom. Generally the major understanding of freedom that concerns people of our time is freedom from domination by someone else, by some other force or power. We tend to look at liberation in terms of an escape from domination. Now one of the things that Jesus has to say to all of us is that freedom *is* ours. Freedom is the most precious gift given to each of us, but not merely to escape domination. Freedom is freedom for being. And perhaps the most important thing in the lives of each person is that we should be free to be ourselves, to respond to the gift of our own creation. In the Christian vision each of us is invited to experience what St Paul called the 'liberty of the children of God'. Not freedom *from* but freedom *for*, for life. For your own life. For the fullness of your life and life in Christ, as a child of God.

Meditation is simply a way of entering into this freedom. It is the freedom that each of us can find if only we will undertake the discipline of the journey. Each of us can find this freedom in our own hearts. But as soon as I use the word discipline, we feel 'Isn't this a loss of freedom?' We cannot help but approach even meditation with our modern indiscipline by saying, 'Okay, I'll try it, I'll see if there's anything in it for me; if there is, I'll stick with it, if there isn't, I'll give it up and try jogging or something else.' However, we can't approach meditation in that way. Even to begin to meditate faces us with the challenge of discipline that it presents to us as modern people because we are not used to doing something unless there is a quick, visible pay off. But meditation is just like breathing. If your life is going to be full, a spiritual discipline is as necessary to your spirit as breathing is to your body. It gives you the necessary space to be, the silence to be and, above all, the peace to be. To be at peace is to experience the reality of a tranquillity and order that is already in your own heart. Of course, this is what everyone is looking for, to be at peace, to be one, to experience, at the centre of your being, your harmony with all beings. That is precisely what meditation is about. But you have to approach it differently from the way you approach everything else. Instead of trying to control or trying to dominate, we have to approach it by letting go and being still. Letting go of your own problems, thoughts and plans is the difficulty that it presents. Now how do you do it? What is involved in meditating? It is utter simplicity.

To meditate you need to, each morning and evening, spend a first few moments just sitting in a comfortable position. If you can sit in the lotus position or the perfect posture that is probably as good a posture as you can find. But it is not essential. It is good to have a comfortable chair to sit on. But choose one with a straight back and a firm seat. If you can meditate just sitting on the floor on a cushion, that too is excellent. It may be necessary to push the cushion up against the wall so you can support your back against the wall. But the important thing is when you have found a comfortable position, then sit absolutely still. This is not easy when you begin, but it is much easier than you may think: just sit still, close your eyes and keep them gently closed. You will find that soon your facial muscles and the other muscles in your body will begin to relax. Then begin to say your mantra. Forget the meaning for the moment. When you begin to meditate you simply listen to the mantra as a sound (*ma-ra-na-tha*). Sound that word in the deepest part of your being, in your heart, and ignore all thoughts, ideas, words and all imagination. The art of meditation is learning to leave behind thought and analysis, words and images and simply to be, to be still, to be one.

We want to be free, we want to experience that liberty in our innermost being. Even a little experience of meditation teaches us about the deep harmony that each person is. The deep harmony that God is. But you have to try it and you can't try a bit of it. You cannot decide to say your word for five minutes to see if anything happens. In meditation nothing happens. You say your word and in that is the act of faith that launches you on the path of enlightenment. In taking it you have to trust yourself to the wisdom of the ages, to the experience of good, simple and wise men and women down through history. And indeed when nothing happens, you can be pretty sure that you are on the right track. And whatever does happen – visions, voices, experiences, whatever else might or might not come into your imagination – you can ignore because it will not be of the slightest importance. What is important is that you learn to be silent. To leave behind all the noise of a distracted mind.

St Paul is one of those wise teachers of the contemplative tradition. In writing to the Galatians his case is that our call as Christians is fully to experience the 'glorious liberty of the children of God'. And he asks how do we achieve that freedom, how do we enter and realize it? He replies, 'The only thing that counts is faith active in love.' And the way to that faith, active in love, is 'union with Christ Jesus'. This is what Christian meditation is about. Jesus dwells in our hearts in a perfect simplicity. Christian meditation is simply allowing his presence to become the supreme reality of our consciousness. To do that we must learn to be silent, to be still and to be attentive to the presence in our hearts. And the way to that attentiveness is to recite our mantra. To recite it from the beginning of our meditation until the end, without ceasing.

The Discipline of Silence

Scripture is a continual source of understanding and inspiration for the Christian pilgrimage and for the way of meditation that makes that pilgrimage a single-minded and unified journey. Consider these words from the Book of Revelation in the light of your daily meditation.

> I heard a loud voice, proclaiming from the throne: Now at last, God has his dwelling among men! He will dwell among them and they shall be his people, and God himself will be with them. He will wipe away every tear from their eyes; there shall be an end to death and to mourning and crying and pain; for the old order has passed away. (Rev. 21:3–4)

We are led to meditate because we are convinced that the old order has passed away and because we are convinced that God does dwell among us. In faith we are convinced that God dwells in our hearts. And if only we will take the trouble and the time, each of us is invited to *find* God in our hearts. Everyone is invited to undertake the journey and then all that is required is that we stay on it.

The quality that everyone of us needs most urgently is silence. We simply must learn how to be silent and how to remain in silence. Once you enter that silence, once you open your heart to that unpredictable and incomparable experience, you will find that each of us can only be the person we are called to be if we allow that silence to develop in our hearts. Make no mistake about it, the silence that each of us is summoned to enter is the eternal silence of God. This is the silence that each of us can find in our own hearts. Discovering it will lead you to understand that silence is itself the medium of perfect communication. It is in silence that we communicate at depth and with the truth of wholeness.

The tradition that we speak from in the monastic order tells us, and quite uncompromisingly, that the way to that silence is a way of discipline. And the discipline is a hard one for us of the twentieth century because we have to learn to leave behind, indeed to abandon, our own thoughts, words, ideas, imagination. That is the silence we need: a silence beyond all words, ideas, thoughts, and beyond all imagination. An ancient tradition tells us that the way to that imageless but wakeful silence, which is the way of meditation, is the way of learning to say, in all simplicity and concentration, our *word*. Our meditation word, our mantra.

There are two particularly important truths to get hold of when you are starting. First, that you must say the word from the beginning to the end – and this is essential to understand. In our tradition there is the basic teaching that you must say the word from the beginning to the end of the meditation period. What often happens is that after saying the word for a bit, you begin to feel very peaceful, perhaps very free. The burden of all your ideas and thoughts has been lifted and then you think, 'This freedom, this peace is rather pleasant, I'll just rest in it. I'll let go of the word, I won't say the word. I'll just enjoy the peace.' That is the high road to disaster. And you will waste a lot of time unnecessarily if you do not learn, at the outset, to say your word from the beginning to the end. Secondly, you must learn to meditate every morning and every evening. Again, make no mistake about that, that is the minimum.

You cannot learn to meditate unless you build it into your life as a regular pattern, as a regular discipline. It requires considerable sacrifice to find that time every morning and evening, indeed considerable discipline. But it is necessary. It is so necessary because the presence of God, in his universe, in his creation, in your heart and my heart, is of such importance that we ignore it at our peril. If we ignore it, we can never make sense of either ourselves or the universe. Because it leads to such meaning, the journey requires seriousness and discipline, which will lead you to a peace and a joy that no words can possibly describe. Silence, you will discover, is the medium of unity. You will discover in the silence of meditation that your outer life and your inner life are unified. That is why bodily stillness is so important. In meditation you will discover body and spirit in *unity*, then in *union* with God. Nothing is more important for people of our time, or indeed of any time, than to recover this capacity for silence.

My recommendation for your daily meditation is to start with a minimum time of twenty minutes. Try as soon as you can to put it to twenty-five; the ideal time is about half an hour. And take the same time, whether it is twenty, twenty-five or thirty minutes – the same time-slot – every day. A practical instruction to remember is that the best time to meditate is before a meal. So, if you can, in the early morning before breakfast and, if you can, in the early evening before supper or dinner.

God is with his people. God dwells in our midst. And that is why we meditate. To be open to his presence. The presence is eternal. Our awakening to it is daily. We awaken to the great Revelation that transforms human consciousness and existence:

> I heard a loud voice proclaiming, now at last, God has his dwelling among men. He will dwell among them and they shall be his people, and God himself will be with them. (Rev. 21:3)

The Unselfish Self

One of life's questions that everybody has to face is, how do we become fully ourselves? How do we become a person in our own right? It is so easy for us merely to try to please our parents or our peers or the aims which the society we live in imposes on us. Yet we know that unless we are fully ourselves, apart from these pressures, we never feel real or authentic people. As you must know from your experience, the only way to become a real person, in your own right, is to establish real relationships with others. And it is in relationships, knowing and being known, that your full self emerges. But before we can enter into any significant relationship, we have to know ourselves and be ourselves. We have to have some sort of understanding of our potential for being, for relationship and for love.

It is this that meditation is about. Meditation is a first step towards establishing the basic human relationship, the relationship with yourself. When you meditate, you do not try to please anyone. You do not try to respond to any role or any image of yourself. Perhaps we all do, to a certain extent, at the beginning. We see ourselves as some holy Buddha, about to levitate maybe. But you soon get over that once you start meditating on a regular daily basis. The romantic understanding of meditation quickly gives way before the experience of the real thing. In fact, it is not only that you give up trying to respond to an image of yourself or someone else's image of yourself, but in meditating you let go of all images. You empty yourself of all images: that is what meditating is about. It is the process of the emptying out of all the fantasy, all the images, all the unreality. So space is made for the real you, the real person you are. Here is a way of looking at meditation: it is a way of making space for yourself to be.

In religious terms people often talk about loving God, loving your neighbour and loving yourself. But I think only a little experience with meditating will show you that the true order is the other way round. You must first learn to be yourself and to love yourself. And secondly you must allow your neighbour to be themselves, and learn to love them. And it is then, and only then, that it makes any sense to talk about God. And indeed, the less you talk and think about God in the initial stages, the better.

Let me remind you how to meditate. You have to learn to say your word, your mantra. The mantra is like one of those signals that keep flashing in the dark, guiding a boat to port or an aircraft to the runway. It flashes in the dark and when you begin meditating you have to say your mantra in the dark. You have to make that act of faith. That this tradition goes back for hundreds of years, that it has been discovered and rediscovered in every century, that this tradition makes sense and that it makes sense for you: all these considerations point towards saying your mantra as a process of freedom. You are freeing yourself from the images, the fantasies, the memories that take away your freedom to be who you are. In the Christian vision of meditation, the whole purpose of this process is to free your spirit to be open to infinity. Allow your heart and your mind, your whole being, to expand beyond all the barriers of your isolated self and to come into union with all. With the All, with God. When you start you will find all sorts of distractions in your mind. The purpose of the mantra is to bring the mind to calm, to peace, to concentration. And the way to do it is to keep saying the mantra. When you first start, you will find that if you say the mantra, continuously, faithfully, then after about ten minutes it will probably bring you to a deep peacefulness. You will be amazed and you will say, 'I had no idea I had this capacity for peace. This is wonderful. I'm just going to hold on to this now and I'm going to stop saying the mantra?' When you do this one of two things happen. You enter into a state of reverie, just floating nowhere, and that's exactly where you are, nowhere. Or your mind is immediately filled again with all sorts of distractions. So when you are starting, be absolutely clear in your mind that the way to meditate is to say your mantra from the beginning to the end. Don't allow any experience of wellbeing that you want to possess or hold on to or any narcissistic approach to prayer that you may be encouraged to adopt, distract you from the truth of the continuous selflessness of the mantra. This is what makes meditating *absolute* simplicity.

Repeat the mantra silently in your heart and keep it going. You will soon find a steady rhythm by which to say it, either with your breathing or with your heartbeat. Do not bother too much about the technicalities when you begin. Say it, recite it, sound it in your heart silently and the mantra will lead you to silence, to discipline, to concentration. If you are faithful to it it will lead you eventually to the bedrock of your own being. Beyond all the roles that you play, behind all the masks by which we hide, beyond all the images which we have of ourselves, we will find the person God creates and loves in eternity.

To learn to meditate, you have to understand that it involves a daily commitment. There are no short cuts. There is no instant mysticism. Meditating is like breathing and eating. It is part of the fabric of daily life. And as breathing and eating strengthen the body, so meditating strengthens the spirit, purifies it and makes it strong.

The Mind of Christ

'We, however, possess the mind of Christ.' (1 Cor. 2:16)

The ongoing pilgrimage of meditation leads us to an ever-deeper encounter with the essential theology of prayer. What does St Paul mean when he says we possess the mind of Christ? We know from the doctrine of the indwelling of the Holy Spirit that the fullness of God is to be found in our own hearts. We know that the full life of the Trinity is lived in our hearts. This is because Jesus Christ dwells in our hearts. His human consciousness is to be found within each of us. The journey of prayer is simply to find the way to open our human consciousness to his human consciousness, and to become, on that way, fully conscious ourselves. The way passes beyond all divided-ness, for there is no longer any subject or object, there is only full consciousness containing both. This is the wonder of the doctrine of the Incarnation. Jesus, being man and possessing a human consciousness, is our way to the Father. Humanly it is possible for us to open our human consciousness to his. That is the marvel, indeed the perfection, of the Christian revelation, that he is the Way, and he is the One Way because his love embraces all human ways. He is the universal Redeemer and the universal Sanctifier. He can be so for us because his human consciousness is fully open to the Father in the Spirit of love. When in the silence of prayer, and the concentration of our meditation, we open our human consciousness to him, we go beyond him, to the Father. We go beyond him by *his* power of self-transcending love.

The way of meditation is the way of opening ourselves as fully as we can in this life to the gift of God. His gift, *par excellence*, is Jesus Christ. He is our light. He is our enlightenment. The fullness of his spirit dwells in our hearts and the task of Christians is to understand this in all its power and wonder in the depth of our spirit. Our gospel, the gospel that we preach, is a gospel of the glory of Christ. A glory that radiates throughout history, and a glory that shines within each of us. The light of that glory is what gives direction to the lives of each one of us. When we meditate every morning and evening we set everything else aside and we are open to that light. We seek to follow that light and so we are illuminated by it. The marvel of meditation is that, if we can be faithful to it, everything in our lives that is not consonant with the light is burned away by it. We do not need to spend time and effort making resolutions to do this or not to do that. All our effort should be put to the single task of coming in to the full consciousness of Jesus. After that effort of faith, everything else is given to us. Everything else in our lives not compatible with the light and warmth of love will fall away, if we will only be faithful to the daily pilgrimage away from division and self-consciousness and into the consciousness of Jesus. Then, just as we must go beyond ourselves into the consciousness of Christ, so he himself takes us beyond himself, in his consciousness, into God, to the Father.

The vision is an intoxicating one. And it is one we can only believe by the experience. The experience is simplicity itself: to devote your half hour in the morning and evening to saying your mantra with absolute fidelity. Shun thoughts and ideas. Shun everything that takes you away from the poverty of that one word. It is the poverty and the humility of meditation proven by your willingness to leave ideas, words and images for the purity of the one word, that is our way into the consciousness of Jesus: 'We, however, possess the mind of Christ.'

For St Paul the mind of Christ we possess is the whole glory of Christ's enlightenment filling us and transforming us. This, not rules and regulations, fears or self-importance, is the gospel:

If indeed our gospel be found veiled, the only people who find it so are those on their way to perdition. Their unbelieving minds are so blinded by the god of this passing age, that the gospel of the glory of Christ, who is the very image of God, cannot dawn upon them and bring them light. It is not ourselves that we proclaim. We proclaim Jesus Christ as Lord and ourselves as your servants for Jesus' sake. For the same God who said – 'Out of darkness let light shine' – has caused his light to shine within us, to give the light of revelation – the revelation of the glory of God in the face of Jesus Christ. (2 Cor. 4:3–6)

That is the wonderful gospel. A gospel that we have to proclaim to the world: that the glory of Christ is to be found in our own hearts. But we can only proclaim it if we *know* it to be true. Each generation of Christians has to accept the personal responsibility of knowing it to be true. The only way that I know that you can respond to that responsibility is by setting out on this journey of silence to your own heart. There to find Christ. There to find yourself opened to his consciousness, and in his consciousness to find yourself, to lose yourself, in the Father.

Open to Prayer

A question that constantly recurs is what are we actually *doing* when we are meditating? What place does it have in our Christian life in general? When you begin meditating and you are told, 'You must say your word from the beginning to the end and you mustn't speak to God or think of God but simply must say your word', you are likely to say, 'But is this prayer? Is it Christian prayer at all? Or is it just some form of relaxation or self-hypnosis?' Now, in the New Testament you find that one of its recurring themes is that prayer is the prayer of Jesus and that it is his prayer that we must learn to be part of. Saying the mantra, saying your word, is simply a *keeping guard* over your heart so that extraneous trivia cannot enter in, even the trivia of your own pious, holy words and thoughts. Nothing must dilute the stream of prayer that is the love of Jesus for his Father. We must be undividedly open to that and the mantra is like a watchdog guarding your heart. That is why you are asked to learn to say it from the beginning to the end of each meditation.

The two dangers you must avoid are, first of all, distraction, not allowing your mind to become involved in trivia. The second is that you must not allow yourself to be just nowhere. Prayer is not just floating in space. It is a full and fully conscious entry into the prayer of Jesus. It is in fact having his mind. As St Paul says, 'We possess the mind of Christ.' One of the constantly recurring themes of the Buddhist scriptures is the warning to humanity not to waste life, not to allow life to slip through our fingers until we suddenly become aware that it is all over. Your life is for living. Your life is for coming to full consciousness, full enlightenment. In the teaching of St Paul, we are allowing the light of Christ to shine with its full brilliance in our heart. The underlying rationale of the Buddhist scriptures is that we must be serious about the purpose of life and not trivialize it or allow it to pass away in an endless series of distractions. As Christians we must be utterly serious in our commitment to the gift that is given us: the gift of life and the gift of redemption. By this we are made one with God in Jesus and as Christians we should be proclaiming this gospel to the whole world saying that each of us is made for this destiny of oneness in fullness of life. That is the essence of the Christian proclamation. We must understand that this is now accomplished in Jesus; if only we will realize it. Meditation is our acceptance of the gift, the gift of life, the gift of Jesus and the self-giving of his Spirit. Because the gift is infinite, it requires our full attention and complete concentration. We are not spending half an hour in the morning and half an hour in the evening going in for a 'bit of religion' or doing spirituality as part of our health programme. In these half hours we seek to live the eternal moment. We seek to set aside everything that is passing away and to live in the eternity of God.

The amazing thing about the Christian proclamation is that we *can* do it, indeed that we are *called* to do it; if only we will be serious. The degree of our seriousness is in direct proportion to the degree we know joy. Because once we realize who we are and what our call is and what has been achieved for us in Jesus, we enter upon an experience of total liberty of spirit. This is what Christianity is about, the full acceptance of that gift of liberty in the truth that we are made free in Christ Jesus. Christianity is not so much obeying this law or that law, fulfilling this obligation or that obligation. It is coming to the whole of life with our hearts filled with wonder at what is, at what has been achieved in Jesus.

But we must be serious. We must be committed. In St Paul's words, we must have *faith*. We must *believe*. As far as I can understand it, the curious thing is that we can only believe and have faith, and so be committed, when we enter into the experience personally: as we let go of our own thoughts and plans and feelings and plunge into the depths of the mystery of God. That is exactly what saying the mantra leads us to. That is why we must say it so faithfully. Allow the thoughts that assail you, and the distractions that come, to fall away. Do not follow them, and do not be discouraged by them. But say your mantra.

Do not be discouraged if you find that you are not saying it, however. If you find that you are caught up in the trivia simply cut loose and return to the mantra. The mantra leads to a peace where we are not tossed around by all the inevitable contingencies of existence. The peace guards our hearts so that, freed from distraction, we can be wholly open to, available to and in the presence of, Christ Jesus in our hearts. In that openness and in our capacity to enter into his consciousness we will never again underestimate the magnificence of the Christian vocation: to enter into the consciousness of Christ and through that entry to know our Father. That is the call for all of us. It is the call for everyone because a common path has been opened up by the life, death and resurrection of Jesus.

St Paul understood the power of the peace of Christ to transform the human condition:

> We by contrast are citizens of Heaven, and from heaven we expect our deliverer to come, the Lord Jesus Christ and he will transfigure the body belonging to our humble state and give it a form like that of his own resplendent body by the very power which enables him to make all things subject to himself. Therefore, my friends, beloved friends whom I long for, my joy, my crown, stand thus firm in the Lord. . . . Then the peace of God which is beyond our utmost understanding will keep guard over your hearts and over your thoughts in Christ Jesus. (Phil. 3:20–4:1, 7)

Recovering Oneness

I was reading an essay recently on the subject of unity. The writer recommended that, if you wanted to understand what is involved in unity, relationship and interdependence, take a good look at one of your hands. You might be tempted to think of your hand just as four fingers and a thumb but, he said, if you look at it closely you will perceive it to be a miracle of beautifully coordinated interdependent relationships. It struck me then that this is one of the great problems of our own time, that the sense of unity has been lost from so much of our life. We so easily divide ourselves into black and white, into artist and artisan, north and south, modern or traditionalist and so forth, that the essential unity, the sense of the brotherhood and sisterhood of the human family, the sense of oneness that is intrinsic to what it means to be human, has been lost. Most of us now know that one of the great problems of modern life is the loss of a sufficiently deep understanding of our oneness with the environment. The danger or consequence of this is that we are living on the edge of an ecological disaster, just because somewhere and somehow we have lost that realistic sense of unity and oneness. In meditation we seek the way towards the basis of all perception of unity, which is the essential oneness that each of us is.

Meditating is utter simplicity. There is absolutely nothing complicated about it at all. It is a oneness of body and spirit and when we sit down to meditate we sit down as a whole person. We do not sit down to engage in some spiritual activity so that ten minutes later we can engage more productively in some secular activity. We sit down as the entire, the whole person that we are – body and spirit – and the purpose of meditation is that, by entering into that unity of our own being,

66

we cease to live life on two, three, four or more levels. We live our life out of the one reality that we are. In this way the religious person can see meditation as a process of sanctification by the Holy Spirit whose gift is unity, who *is* the unity of the Tri-personal God. We are called to be holy as God is holy. This means to be one as God is one, to be unified in relationship.

In the Christian vision each of us is on a pilgrimage to discover that the wonder of our own creation is that we are created by God for an eternal destiny, for an infinite expansion of spirit. What we have to learn when we meditate is some glimmer of an insight into our own value and importance. If God has sent his Son, Jesus, to reveal both his greatness and our potential, this is the basis of seeing our infinite value. Seeing it is the perception of faith and we learn in meditation that the source of faith is the Spirit of Jesus dwelling in our heart. Now, we know these propositions as statements of theological theory, but if we want to live the fullness of our life in the fullness of Christian faith, which is one and the same, then we have to uncover these truths as existent realities in our heart. And that is what meditation is about: uncovering the truth that reveals reality.

Truth is about body *and* spirit and so the first thing we have to learn when we begin to meditate is to sit still. As Westerners we can become technically over-concerned with posture. We may like the image of ourselves in certain stereotyped poses. Posture is *not* about posing and the only essential rules about posture are that the spine is as upright as possible and that you sit as still as possible. But this reveals a discipline that every one of us must learn. We are not used to sitting still. We are not used to being mentally still. But the spirit must come to stillness in a profound unity with the body that rests in profound stillness. You will find out from your own experience that bodily stillness is not the most difficult form of stillness. More demanding is the stillness of mind involved in our going beyond imagining, reasoning, comparing, analysing and judging. One of the greatest hazards we face in meditation is as a result of our over-intellectualist education. In meditating we are not thinking about God or analysing reality. We are being still and learning to know his essence; learning, that is, how to learn.

We come to see that he is love and, in a true sense, meditating is simply uncovering the love that is God in our own hearts. The way that our tradition teaches us to approach this self-revelation of God is not to think, to analyse or to reason but to learn to be like a little child, to learn to be humble. This we do by the simple and constant repetition of our word. So to meditate we need to sit still and to sit upright. To begin with you will want to scratch your nose or your ear but you must go through that. Just sit still. Then you must learn to say your word.

You will find as you go on that you can be saying your mantra at one level while at another level there are thoughts going on below and at another level above, at another on one side, at another on the other side. Ignore them all. Say your mantra. That is the art of meditating: to say your word in the silent eye of the storm.

The mystery of meditation is that you are led to the experience of stillness, of unity by the mantra which is just like God's harmonic sounding in your heart. It leads you into an experience of unity – unity within yourself, body and spirit, unity with all creation. As you sit meditating you are in your place in the universe and meditation leads you into the personal experience that God is the centre of the universe. This is what the daily practice – the daily practice is essential – will lead you to, in all gentleness. You can't learn to meditate by reading books about meditation or by listening to talks on meditation. You can only learn to meditate by meditating, every day, every morning and every evening. Do not let yourself be discouraged. To begin with you will find that you miss a morning or an evening (or a day or a week or a month). But if you have understood, even dimly, what is involved in the practice of meditation you will return to it to learn how essential it is to enter into that depth of your spirit every single day of your life. Meditation is about freedom, liberty of spirit, expansion of spirit. But the way is, to us as modern people, surprising because it is a way of discipline.

In the Letter to the Ephesians St Paul explores the deep structural unity between redemption and unity:

For in Christ our release is secured and our sins are forgiven through the shedding of his blood and therein lies the richness of God's grace freely lavished upon us imparting full wisdom and insight. He has made known to us his hidden purpose. Such was his will and pleasure determined beforehand in Christ to be brought into effect when the time was ripe, namely that the universe, all in heaven and all on earth, might be brought into a unity in Christ. (Eph. 1:7–10)

If you are going to meditate now do so in the faith that that is our purpose, to come into full unity in Christ.

Real Knowing

One of the countless benefits that we have to gain from meditation is that we are empowered to transcend the cultural context in which we have been brought up. All of us are, to some extent, prisoners of the received ideas of our time and as a result we are distressed to find so little creativity in our thinking. People are almost afraid to think their own thoughts. Everyone merely shuffles with the pack of ideas that we have had presented to us, not even, I'm afraid, by the true thinkers of our time, but often just by the prepackagers of secondhand, convenience-concepts. In the silence of meditation we are put in touch with our own uniqueness and we are given the courage to be ourself, to know ourself and the world we inhabit, to think and respond to a real world first-hand. It is about direct knowledge that I would like to reflect a little in the light of meditation.

Many years ago I attended the school of Oriental and African studies in London. I remember being appalled as I walked into the school on my first day and read the motto over the door: Knowledge is Power. This is one of the popular, uncritically accepted ideas that effect us all today. Without reflection we think of knowledge in terms of power. But compare this idea of knowledge with St Paul's concept of *gnosis*.

> I pray that the God of our Lord Jesus Christ, the all glorious Father, may give you the spiritual powers of wisdom and vision, by which there comes the knowledge (*gnosis*) of him. I pray that your inward eyes may be illumined, so that you may know what is the hope to which he calls you. (Eph. 1:17–18)

For Paul knowledge is not power, as though to know God

is to have power over him, or as though knowing God gives us power over others. The only 'power' he talks of is that of wisdom and vision, gifts not tools, which lead to authentic knowledge. Personal knowledge of someone is not only objective. To know someone is not knowing something *about* them, which might give you power over them. Knowing someone is to be in harmony with them. The Hebrew word to *know* is the same as the word to *love*. Knowing is to be one with. To be lost in the other is necessary in order fully to know the other. When you know the other and know yourself to be known, *then* you know. Knowledge is not only not power, it is more than power. It is surrender, being at one with, going beyond one's limitations into union. To seek power is to find only *my* power whereas to seek knowledge as love is to discover my self one with a reality greater than I am alone.

This is what we have to learn in meditation, but learning requires humility. Even in the early Church the Gnostics thought that their knowledge would somehow or other give them power. But if it is true to say that knowledge is power, then it is only the power to love. The power to lose one's self, the courage to lose one's self, is the gift enjoyed by the humble and the silent.

Meditation is our acceptance of this challenge. The mantra accepts the human challenge to know God, to know him without fear and to know him to the fullness of our capacity to know. To rise to the adventure of life, our meditation requires not part of our attention or part of our love, but the whole of our attention and the unified intention of our love. And so, we learn to say the mantra with complete fidelity and with total attention. To learn this art of prayer, as to learn anything, we must be prepared to be patient, because to learn fidelity and full attention requires continual patience. The knowledge we come to in meditation is not merely new additions to the memory bank. The knowledge we come to is wisdom. Wisdom is to know the significance of what we know, to know in perspective and true proportion. Wisdom is simply knowing with a divine perspective; it means knowing everything we are given to know in the perspective of eternity. We know what is important when we know what it is that endures forever. Wisdom is

71

the fruit of growth in meditation because we know with certain knowledge that God is, and that he is eternal. And that he is eternal Love. The seed of new growth which is generated by the fruit of meditation is charity. In the silence of meditation we know that the well-spring of God's eternal love overflows into our own hearts. To know that, we need only the simplicity, the wise childlikeness to say our word and to continue saying it, every morning and every evening. Perseverance is our way into the knowledge that is harmony, that is one and one-ing. Whatever power we may have is given us 'from above', that is through our true knowledge of our oneness with Christ.

> I pray that your inward eyes may be illumined, so that you may know what is the hope to which he calls you, and what the wealth and glory of the share he offers you and how vast the resources of his power open to us who trust in him. They are measured by his strength and might which he exerted in Christ, when he raised him from the dead and when he enthroned him at his right hand in the heavenly realms, far above all government and authority, all power and dominion and any title of sovereignty that can be named, not only in this age but in the age to come. He put everything in subjection beneath his feet and appointed him as supreme head to the Church which is his Body, and as such holds within it the fullness of him who himself receives the entire fullness of God. (Eph. 1:18–23)

In meditating we open our hearts and our minds in purified consciousness to that fullness. We open to love. The love which is the energy of the Godhead, of the universe, is also the energy of life which flows in the heart of each one of us.

The Non-mechanics of the Pilgrimage

The teaching of Jesus on prayer in the gospel is the basic teaching underlying meditation. For example, the spirit of faithful trust implicit in the mantra is what we find in his injunction to 'Set your mind on God's kingdom and his justice before everything else and all the rest will come to you as well.' Today especially, I think, many people are perplexed as to what is involved in the spiritual option in life presented in these words and accepted in meditation. You can't help, in our very materialistic society, but say what is there in this for me? If I follow the spiritual path, what am I going to get out of it? Just consider the basic concepts of life that we have in our society. The basic model we operate on is an essentially mechanistic one and life can easily become a mechanical operation. We think we are learning to deal with life by mastering the procedures and as a result we miss the vitality of experience.

A few years ago when I was headmaster of a school in the United States, I was horrified to receive a letter from the department of education saying that there was a shortage of engineers, and as many students as possible should therefore be directed into subjects that would qualify them for engineering studies at university. There you have a whole concept of education which is seen merely as programming people, just as you would program a machine, so that individuals can become efficient cogs in the larger machine of society. This is why it is so important that we seriously awaken to the spiritual potential that we all have. It is not only our minds that will suffer if we do not. We even tend, in this mechanistic view, to view our bodies as machines that have to be properly serviced.

Meditation is important because we must free ourselves from this mechanistic view of ourselves and of society. Spiritually it

73

is of supreme importance because it is the most practical step that any one can take to rediscover himself, not as a machine or as a mechanistic cog in some vast assembly line, but in order to come to know ourselves as possessing an infinite depth of mystery. It is of supreme importance that every one of us make this discovery for ourselves. We can't take someone else's word for it. It is something that each of us must know, and know fully and clearly, from our own experience. Once we do know it, everything else follows from it in right order.

In discovering that potential, that depth of spirit within ourselves, we also take the first step in discovering that those we live with, those we love, those we work with, all possess this same depth of spirit, the same capacity for opening to the mystery of their own being. We can hardly dare to imagine what a society would be like where everybody was on the road to the realization that being is mystery, that each of us possess an infinite capacity, an infinite potential for expansion of the spirit into the mystery of God. And yet we *should* dare to imagine that: we should dare to imagine that it is possible for a society to exist where compassion takes precedence over judgment, where mercy and forgiveness are the regular currency. But compassion, mercy, forgiveness and love all depend upon that discovery of ourselves and others to be more than machines. This discovery will mean seeing society not as some anonymous body that needs servicing but as a community of persons committed to maturity, to growth, to understanding, to love. But that society cannot be, unless men and women can be found who will undertake the pilgrimage to the bedrock of their own being, who will be prepared to undertake the discipline of discovering their own infinite depths, their infinite capacity for love, for understanding: for God. But it is useless even to talk about God unless the commitment to that journey of self-discovery is there too.

More and more people who have been meditating for some years are now awakening to the community of silent love they share. I want to remind you again of the importance of the discipline that is involved. The journey is away from self and beyond self, into the infinity of God. The journey is away from all egoism. In the words of Jesus, 'No one can be a follower of mine, unless he leave self behind.' It is surprising to discover that the first step in self-transcendence is to be still. In meditation this asks us to learn the discipline of sitting still. In that stillness the body becomes an outward sign of the inward stillness that you approach in your pilgrimage of the mantra. Even as you become a committed meditator, do not underestimate the importance of an upright, alert posture and of absolute stillness. Both contribute to the preparation for that inward stillness wherein the mystery unfolds itself. The journey of meditation is a journey into the mystery of being. It is a journey in which we discover our own mystery as part of the infinite mystery.

The way remains one of absolute simplicity. There is no advanced technique involved or any complicated books that you need to read. The most simple person can undertake this journey. Indeed, the simpler the better to begin with. All you need for the journey is discipline, commitment to the daily return to it and to making that space in your day and in your heart. And you need faith. The basic faith you need is that you *are*, that you are valuable and that you are valued. This is the faith that you are lovable and that you are loved. You need this faith when you begin and as you continue on the pilgrimage your faith will grow, your fears will fall away. The maturing of faith and the falling away of fear depend on your commitment to the mantra, which is another way of saying your determination to leave self behind and to journey into the mystery.

Reverence

It is always useful to reflect on the final part of the explanation of the parable of the sower in the Gospel of Luke. The seed which fell in good soil represents all those who bring a good and honest heart to the hearing of the Word, who hold it fast and, by their perseverance, yield a rich harvest. Perhaps the most important value for us to recover in our society is this fruitful reverence in the presence of mystery. To know the holiness of God, the wonder of his purposes, and recognizing this, to be in-formed with reverential awe is basic to pure religion. And to recover the value of reverence we need space and silence. So many people in our world are in such a state of emotional exhaustion that they can experience nothing in depth, or perhaps the only thing they can experience is anaesthesia. In the face of exhaustion by shallowness, maybe we should not be surprised that so many people in our society actively look for the experience of anaesthesia.

We need to approach the tradition of meditation with reverence. Even to hear of this tradition is a very great grace for each one of us. I count it myself as the greatest grace in my life. Then to encounter it as a living tradition, as a living experience in people, is an even greater grace. And again, I count it as the greatest grace in my own life that I learned to pray in the presence of a very holy man. What he taught me so evidently came from his own experience that I learned more in one half hour of meditation in silence with him than I have learned from all the books and articles that I have read since. It is the greatest grace for each of us to find the way to enter the living stream of prayer within our own hearts.

The first effect of this entry is to awaken us to ourselves. We all discover as a consequence of meditation that we can only fully know ourselves if we enter with courage into that other living stream that is the human family. In other words, it is only by entering into the experience of otherness that we can become ourselves. This is true at every level of our lives: emotional, intellectual, psychological, spiritual. We recognize our own humanity, our capacity for love, for being and for joy, only as the result of a deep understanding of our relationships. What we are is a fusion of where we came from, where we are and where we are journeying to. We know ourselves fully only when we recognize that we are on the journey, with others, to the Other. And I think what we can learn in our meditation is that our selfhood is in proportion to our experience of otherness. Put it another way, the degree to which we experience our selfhood will be the degree to which we have experienced otherness. That means, how far we have gone beyond our own limited experience and entered into the experience of the tradition of the human family and, beyond that, into the experience of Christ, and beyond that into God. The challenge to each of us in this vision is to listen to the tradition and to follow the tradition.

It requires humility to follow anything or anyone. But it is the only true wisdom, to be humble. We must never evade the call to leave self utterly behind; to go beyond all self-conscious thought and follow through into the mystery of the otherness of God. If, once we hear the word that calls us we evade the call to follow, we in fact evade ourselves. And not only ourselves, but all reality. This is the ultimate human tragedy, the tragedy of unauthenticity, of falseness, of always living at one remove from reality. At best, this must almost inevitably lead to appalling sadness and, at worst, to a consuming bitterness.

Meditation is a universal means to lead us to reality. The reality that we are, the reality that our neighbour is, the reality that history is and the ultimate reality, the reality that is God. Meditation is the means open to everyone who would encounter the Spirit in their own heart. And so I want to encourage each one of you to persevere in meditation. Courage is what we need, the courage above all to abandon all images, especially the images that we have of ourselves, which are the principle stumbling block. The way to abandon all those images is to say our word with deepening fidelity. To enter into our own selfhood is to enter into God. This is the call given to each one of us, to know ourselves in God. It is an astonishing destiny and it has been given to us in Jesus to know that destiny. Our life's task is to respond to it, in utter seriousness and with total joy. So listen to the word of the tradition. Hold fast to it and reap the harvest of eternal love. That is the good news of the Gospel. Listen to St Luke again:

> The seed in good soil represents those who bring a good and honest heart to the hearing of the Word, hold it fast, and by their perseverance yield a harvest. (Lk. 8:15)

Growing in God

It is very difficult to try to determine what it is that makes a person want to meditate. It has puzzled me over the years. There seem to be so many reasons why people start to meditate. But I think there is only one reason that keeps people meditating. That I think we could describe as a growing commitment to reality.

The longer you meditate, the longer you persevere through the difficulties and the false starts, then the clearer it becomes to you that you *have* to continue if you are going to lead your life in a meaningful and profound way. You must never forget the way of meditation: to say your mantra from the beginning to the end. This is basic, axiomatic and let nothing dissuade you from the truth of it. In your reading you may come across all sorts of variants and alternatives. But the discipline, the ascesis of meditation places this one demand on us absolutely: that we must leave self behind so completely, leave our thoughts, analyses and feelings behind so completely, that we can be totally at the disposition of the Other. We must do so in an absolute way and that is the demand that the mantra makes upon us: to say it from beginning to the end, in all simplicity and in absolute fidelity.

What is the difference between reality and unreality? I think one way we can understand it is to see unreality as the product of desire. One thing we learn in meditation is to abandon desire, and we learn it because we know that our invitation is to live wholly in the present moment. Reality is simply being grounded in God, the ground of our being. Desire demands constant movement, constant striving. Reality demands stillness and silence. And that is the commitment that we make in meditating. As everyone can find from their own experience, we learn in the stillness and silence to accept ourselves as we are. This sounds very strange to modern ears, above all to modern Christians who have been brought up to practice so much anxious striving: 'Shouldn't I be ambitious? What if I'm a bad person, shouldn't I *desire* to be better?'

The real tragedy of our time is that we are so filled with desire, for happiness, for success, for wealth, for power, whatever it may be, that we are always imagining ourselves as we *might* be. So rarely do we come to know ourselves as we *are* and to accept our present position.

But the traditional wisdom tells us: know that you are and that you are as you are. It may well be that we are sinners and if we are, it is important that we should know that we are. But far more important for us is to know from our own experience that God is the ground of our being and that we are rooted and founded in him. Each of us must know that personally, from our own experience, in our own hearts. This is the stability that we all need, not the striving and movement of desire but the stability and the stillness of spiritual rootedness. Each of us is invited to learn in our meditation, in our stillness in God, that in him we have everything that is necessary.

The root from which we are sprung is Love. In God we are and we know ourselves to be lovable and loved. This is the supreme reality that Jesus came to reveal, to communicate, to live and to establish. It is established in our hearts if only we will be open to it. This openness is what our meditation is about. It is only from this love and with this love that we can rightly understand ourselves and all creation. Without rootedness in love all we can see will be shadows and phantoms and we will never be able to make contact with them because they have no reality. Meditation is the invitation to journey deeply into your own heart, into your own being. What the traditional wisdom tells us is that only with such depth of experience and vision can we live our lives in real harmony with what is. This is what meditation leads us to: the understanding from our own experience simply that God is.

Meditation is the supreme way into faith, into commitment. All action must be shallow, mere immediacy, if it is not based on this commitment to what is real, which must also be to what

80

is eternal. Our invitation as Christians is to know now, with direct, personal knowledge, what is real and eternal and, knowing it, to live our lives inspired by love. This call lies behind these words of Jesus in the Gospel of John:

If a man aims at honour of Him who sent me he is sincere and there is nothing false in him. (Jn 7:18)

The purpose of our meditation is that there should be nothing false in us, only reality. Only love. Only God.

Stillness

Especially when you are starting to meditate it is extremely important to approach meditation with absolute clarity as to what is involved. When I learned to meditate I had a teacher who put it before me with crystal clarity. His teaching was summed up in three words: say your mantra. In the last thirty years I have been increasingly impressed by the extraordinary wisdom of his teaching. Saying the mantra is the first thing to understand. It may take you five or ten years to understand the importance of saying your mantra from the beginning to the end of your meditation, without ceasing. You will meet alternative doctrines but I would urge you to stay with the tradition which tells us that if we would find a central reality, then we must learn to be deeply silent. We must learn to be disciplined and we must learn to leave our thoughts and imagination entirely behind. The faithful recitation of the mantra is the way. It takes time to learn the wisdom and deep truthfulness of this radically simple teaching. As I say, it has taken me a good part of thirty years to understand the importance of it.

There is another important preliminary lesson in learning to meditate: the necessity for stillness. You must learn to be completely still during the meditation. That means, when you sit down choose a really alert posture, with your spine upright; place your arms and hands in a comfortable position, palms upright or facing down with thumb and forefinger joined. Then stay absolutely still. The temptation will come to scratch your nose or straighten your collar or tie or glasses. You will have all sorts of longings to stroke your beard, if you have one, or to rearrange your hair, if you have any.

If you are young enough and your bones are supple enough,

you might try some kind of cross-legged position with the spine upright and the whole body peacefully together in a traditional posture, the perfect or lotus posture, for example. When you are beginning this, you may encounter a certain amount of physical discomfort, as well as the urge to scratch your nose. But you have to try to go through that as well as you can. If you are learning to sit in the lotus position, it would be wise to practise outside of meditation and then to sit in an ordinary alert cross-legged position to begin with and not undertake the lotus position during meditation until you have some proficiency in it. Alternatively, choose a chair with a straight back and a comfortable angle for arms and legs. Chair or floor is not of the greatest importance but the posture and stillness is of supreme importance. Posture is an outward sign of your inner commitment to the discipline of meditation.

Stillness is the way to rootedness and it focuses the challenge that faces all of us, to be rooted in our true self. To put it another way, it is the challenge to be wholly open to the gift of our own creation. Stillness helps us to be rooted in the gift that God has given us in our own being, which we learn by being still in the one place. Coming in to our own selfhood is coming into God. What you will discover in your meditation is the reciprocal harmony that we have with God. Becoming rooted in ourselves, we become rooted in our own proper place in creation and, as a result, rooted in our Creator. St Paul constantly reminds us that the challenge and the task of life is to become 'rooted in Christ', who dwells in our hearts. This is why we have to become rooted in our own hearts. Outward silence and stillness are an effective sign of the inner stillness and silence of inner rootedness. Do not underestimate this as a challenge for people of our time. We have become so much a rootless people that we have lost the sense of our own identity. As a part of this condition we have lost the sense of harmony with God and with creation. It is urgent for us all that we return to ourselves, to our rootedness. Meditation soon takes us beyond a narrow view of personal salvation and makes us aware of our inter-relatedness with the whole family of humanity.

Meditation is a discipline. It is the discipline of the disciple open to the Master, alert, present and reverent as we come into his presence. Meditation is becoming wholly present in the now, that is, the eternal moment of God. Meditation is simply the full acceptance of that reality in discipline, in faithfulness and in love.

And so, whether you are meditating on your own at home or with a group, be still. Be as still as you can be. Be open to God's gift to you. The gift of your own being and the gift of his Spirit who dwells in your heart. St Paul wrote to Timothy:

> Never be ashamed of your testimony to our Lord, nor of me his prisoner, but take your share of suffering for the sake of the gospel, in the strength that comes from God. It is he who brought us salvation and called us to a dedicated life, not for any merit of ours but of his own purpose and his own grace, which was granted to us in Christ Jesus from all eternity, but has now at length been brought fully into view, by the appearance on earth of our Saviour Jesus Christ. For he has broken the power of death and brought life and immortality to light, through the gospel. (2 Tim. 1:8–10)

This is the context within which we meditate today. In the light and life of Jesus.

Why is Meditation Difficult?

I was talking to someone the other day and they were saying to me, 'If this meditation is so obvious and if it should be so natural for all of us and if, as you say, this is what we were created for, why is it so difficult? If it were something that was absolutely natural for each of us, then why should we find it so difficult to sit down, to sit still and to say our mantra for half an hour?' I am sure you will recognize that this is quite a good question to be concerned about; why *should* it be so difficult? It isn't much comfort to such a person to say the difficulty is only illusory; in fact, it is really quite simple!

I think it *is* true to say, however, that if you want to follow this pilgrimage you have to rethink most of your basic religious ideas. I was reading a book recently written by a contemporary nun and I was astonished in reading it for I constantly had to re-edit almost everything she said. I think I knew what she meant but her language jarred on almost every page. I was reading her account of the necessity for the desire for God, and yet it seems to me that we must have no desire for God. Desire is the very enemy of prayer because when we pray we enter so totally into the mystery of God that there is no 'I' to desire. There is only God, and we only know ourselves in him.

I think one of the concepts that can help us to understand the absoluteness of saying the mantra, the absoluteness of the experience of meditation, is the concept of destiny. Prayer, we could perhaps describe as the state of obediential love. The state wherein we are wholly at God's disposition, not desiring, not planning but simply placing ourselves within the fullness of his gift of life, the fullness of his gift of our own unique creation. And each one of us is created for a unique destiny, a unique fulfilment in God and our only task in life is to be wholly open to that destiny. In other words, our task is to live out of the divine energy, to live within the divine plan and to play our part in it fully and generously. You may have been meditating long enough to know that prayer has very little to do with asking for this or asking for that. Prayer is something much more simple than that. It is being at one with God. Why is it so difficult?

I think it is so difficult for us as men and women of the twentieth century because we live in such a materialistic society. It is a society that sees everything in terms of possession and possessing and, even if we happen to be more spiritual in our outlook, we can easily become spiritual materialists. Instead of accumulating money we try to accumulate grace or merit. But the way of prayer is the way of dispossession and of surrender, and that is hard for us because we have been taught success, we have been taught the importance of winning, not losing. But Jesus tells us that if we would find our life we must lose it. And saying our mantra is exactly our response to that command of Jesus to be wholly at his disposition, to give him our undivided attention, to give him our undivided heart, to be in the state of undivided consciousness, which is another way of saying to be at one with him.

Meditation does call for generosity because it calls for everything. It calls for that abandonment of desire and desiring and, positively, it calls for generous openness to God's destiny for us, to his plan for us, to his love for us. What you discover in meditation is just that – his love for you. So many people when they hear about meditation for the first time think of it as some extraordinarily dry, intellectual, unemotional, unaffective way. But it is none of those things. It is commitment to and openness to infinite love, and that love is like a mighty fountain bursting through in your heart. The mantra is like the needle of a compass. It heads you always in the direction of your own destiny. It points always to the true direction you must follow, away from self into God and, whichever way your ego may lead you, the compass is always faithful in the direction it points you. The mantra, if you say it with generosity, with faithfulness and with love will always point you in the direction of God and it is only in God that our true destiny can be revealed.

Listen to St Paul as he puts before the early Christians the essence of the Christian way:

> Finally then, find your strength in the Lord, in his mighty power. Put on all the armour which God provides so that you may be able to stand firm against the devices of the devil. Take up God's armour; then you will be able to stand your ground when things are at their worst, to complete every task and still to stand. Stand firm I say. Buckle on the belt of truth; for coat of mail put on integrity and let the shoes on your feet be the gospel of peace, to give you firm footing; and with all these, take up the good shield of faith. Take salvation for a helmet; for sword take that which the Spirit gives you. Give yourselves wholly to prayer. Pray on every occasion in the power of the Spirit. (Eph. 6:10–11, 13–18)

That is what our meditation is about – openness to God's power, to his love, openness to his plan for each of us, as the whole universe is brought into unity in Christ.

Meditation as Conversion

For St Benedict one of the principal qualities needed in a truly Christian life was what he described as an ongoing conversion. It is helpful and necessary to think about meditation as this process of continual conversion.

Benedict saw the Christian life not in terms of an intellectual assent to certain propositions but much more as a lifelong and wholehearted commitment to the truth. In his vision, true conversion had necessarily to involve the whole person and living a complete life. I think we, too, need to understand conversion as a coming to completion in the light of God. It is a process of enlightenment and, coming into God's light, we cease to have the searchlight of consciousness trained on ourselves. Our consciousness is converted as it is turned towards God and we realize that the searchlight is always *his* light. Every time we meditate we enter with more commitment into this movement of conversion, and so discover more clearly what it is. Conversion is to the spiritual life what revolution or reform is to political life. It is the principle that ensures freshness, honesty and integrity, and the best revolutions are peaceful. They occur in societies that recognize the necessity for change and this change is peacefully embraced by an orderly, constitutional process.

In the spiritual life the same sort of principles apply. We do not need to approach conversion with any sort of dramatic histrionics. What we all need is the daily, orderly return to the process, the due process of the spiritual law; the process whereby our angle of vision is altered so that we can clearly see the basis of all sovereignty, so that we know from our own knowledge and conviction that Jesus is Lord. By daily conversion we learn to live, not out of our moods or the ebb and flow of emotion, not out of our theories or feelings, but to have moods, emotion, thought and feelings enlightened by the pure, steady light of God. It is, therefore, sometimes said that conversion means learning to live by the will of God, rather than by our own will. In a certain sense this is true enough. But I think what we discover in meditation is that conversion is much more the process of learning to *see* as God sees. That is, learning to see not just on the surface but from the depths. It is, in the same way, the process of learning to love as God loves. Learning all this is the very basis of our being.

Why meditation is important for all of us is that, in order to enter this all-important process of conversion, to change our angle of vision and learn to love, we have to make certain significant readjustments. We have to adjust to the fact that God is the ground and centre of all being. We have to adjust to God as the centre of *our* being and so we have to accept that we can only be truly ourselves in him. There is no human being who does not need to learn that we have to abandon all the compromises we have made with the truth, and to see and know that our destiny is to come into the full light of his love. Only in that light will we ever be able to know who we are, what reality is, who God is. It is the primary destiny of each of us to come to that knowledge, to come to that self-authenticating truth, the liberating truth about ourselves, about him, about all that is. Meditation is of such supreme importance because it is in the power of the field of his presence that we learn that we have nothing to fear in coming to the truth about ourselves. We have nothing at all to fear from past or future events. In coming to the truth about all reality we learn that we have nothing to fear in coming to the truth about God, for we learn that God is truth itself and is unfailing compassion, almighty gentleness, rectifying forgiveness. Meditation is the traditional and simple process whereby we learn to leave all fears behind because they are cast out by a truth-filled love. And meditation is a pure opening of the heart, a *being energized* by God's infinite love.

Christians are known to talk a great deal about sin. The really important thing to know is that if we are sinners (and all of us should know that we are) our sins are of no account.

They cannot exist because they are entirely blotted out in the light of God's love. In that light they simply are not. And this is the confidence that all of us need if we are to respond to the vision of Christian life, the vision proclaimed by Jesus. We need to respond to that vision with supreme confidence in the power of redemption, in the power of our ongoing salvation, in the power of his ever-active love. We need, in short, to wake up. 'Awake sleeper, rise from the dead and Christ will shine upon you' (Eph. 5:14). Waking up means opening the eye of the heart to what Benedict calls the 'divinizing light'. What we see in and by that light transforms, converts who we are; and each time we meditate we take a further step into this light which is a new life. Meditation comes to put an end to all the dullness, the fear, the pettiness, all the lack of love in our lives as we return to it each morning and each evening, with an absolute seriousness and deepening joy. The test of our seriousness is that we say the mantra from the beginning to the end, leaving self behind, leaving thoughts behind and journeying into the light. The test of our joy is the new life our ongoing conversion releases.

> But everything, when once the light has shown it up, is illumined, and everything thus illumined is all light. And so the hymn says, 'Awake sleeper, rise from the dead and Christ will shine upon you'. . . . Let the Holy Spirit fill you . . . and in the name of our Lord Jesus Christ give thanks every day for everything to our God and Father. (Eph. 5:13–14, 18, 20)

When we meditate we place ourselves entirely within the ambience of wakefulness to that light. In the silence of meditation we open our hearts to the light, which is the life and power of Christ. What we must remember is to be faithful to saying our mantra from beginning to end.

Eternal Youth

One of the myths that is most deeply rooted in the human psyche is the myth of eternal youth. In our society though, one of the greatest fears and sources of sadness among people is the fear of aging and declining physical powers. The sadness arises because the aging process leads us to believe that the dream of eternal youth is an illusion. Instead of the certainty that there exists a spring of eternal youth always replenishing us with freshness and vigour, we are forced to accept the conclusion that we have only a very limited store of energy that quickly reaches its peak and then sets into a period of long decline.

As we meditate, we discover that the myth of eternal youth contains and expresses a profound truth about the human condition. What we all need, whatever our age, is the wisdom to discover the path to this energy of eternal youth. The spring that the myth describes is hidden deep in a thick forest and the journey through the forest is full of difficulties and ordeals. But the journey symbolizes an interior journey, an interior process of reality. As we all sadly discover, if we search for the spring of eternal youth in externals alone we will unearth only the disappointment of mortality. But if we search within, embracing the discipline and rigour of the journey, we find far more quickly than we might imagine that the spring that Jesus speaks of does exist. The 'spring of living water welling up to eternal life' within us is most certainly there for all of us to approach and for all of us to drink deeply from. If we are making this interior journey to the spring within us then, as we grow older, we do become more childlike.

From time to time, we meet older people who are radiant with all the simplicity of children. They possess spontaneity, openness, freedom and freshness along with the serenity and wisdom of experience. It is this combination of innocence and experience that we call maturity, Christian maturity. One of the characteristics of such maturity is that the person possessing it can be reached, can be touched. The child and the wise man or woman are both reachable, touchable. A child possesses this innocence naturally. Most of us, unfortunately, lose it because we have been hurt or disappointed, or because we so feel that we have been betrayed that it seems there is no chance of risking ourselves again to the free-flowing communication arising from such innocence. We feel we would be mistreated or misunderstood. As a result, we become not wise but cynical. It is not often a sought-after cynicism, nor even a voluntary cynicism but an orientation that we see rising more and more strongly within us, and often we see its approach fearfully. Instead of being reachable and reached by others in deepening sensitivity, we find ourselves becoming hardened; we become callous where we have been wounded and then we build up defences around ourselves to protect our woundedness, our vulnerability.

It is often somewhere in this stage that we start to meditate. Some more fortunate people might start to meditate while still in the stage of innocence, but most begin with a sense of having lost something that they must recover. Often we have an urgent sense that our essential survival depends on our finding our way back to that innocence. The marvel of the journey within however is that we recover something much greater than what was lost. The wonder of the Christian message and its vision of the journey is its proclamation that we recover not just our own lost innocence, but the innocence of Christ. Our new innocence is what he recovered for all mankind, through the cross, through the resurrection. The path back to the spring of eternal life may be demanding but on the way we follow the stream that flows directly from the spring. And so, even on the journey itself we are given all the refreshment and all the guidance we need.

Meditation is our way onto the path. The Spirit is the stream flowing within our hearts. The mantra is the implement that clears the way through the impenetrable forest. We must simply stay on the journey and we must be faithful to the recitation of the mantra. We must never settle for half clarity, for half enlightenment. Our call is to come into the full light of Christ, and it is a call given to each one of us to grow to that maturity and full stature which is nothing less than the full, immortal life of Christ.

So shall we all at last attain to the unity inherent in our faith and our knowledge of the Son of God – to mature manhood, measured by nothing less than the full stature of Christ. (Eph. 4:13)

Worship in Spirit

When you start to meditate you hope that it is going to be a great help in your life. I suppose most of us then keep going because, in ways we perhaps did not imagine, it proves to be practical; it helps us. When we start to meditate, however, we should also be clear about the challenge that meditation will pose for us as we continue. At a certain point I think we are all tempted to give up. We are unsettled by the absolute nature of what appears, both of the mystery of God itself, and even by the absolute nature of the path of meditation. In the encounter with the absolute we are tempted to hold back. We like to hang on to our familiar illusions. All of us, too, like to keep our options open. The best way to understand this inner contradiction is by reference to the ego. The ego is the father of lies, a prince of illusions. It is the ego who casts all the characters in our consciousness in their various roles. And the directing power of the ego remains unbroken as long as we are enchained to what is passing away by desire or regret which are both forms of possessiveness, forms of *being possessed*.

The challenge that each of us has to face in life is to become wholly committed to what is eternal. As soon as we begin to live our lives with what endures as our essential reference point, the ego's power begins to wane. And so the essential challenge to face and meet is to root and found our lives on eternal, enduring reality. And this is God.

We will discover as we persevere in meditation that we cannot put God on hold, keep him in a waiting room and say to him, 'When I'm through with this important business I'm so absorbed in, I'll attend to you.' We cannot postpone God and say 'I'll be back in a minute.' As we commit ourselves to meditate every morning and evening we see the central significance of God's eternal presentness and we recognize that we have to learn to pay attention to God now, today. This is what causes us a minor panic, because we wonder *will we be able to do it*? But there is really no cause for panic. Indeed the only cause for panic would be the reverse, if we had no encounter with the truth of God's presence and the need of response on our part. We ought to panic if we realize that we are deciding to commit ourselves to what is passing away, to the second rate, to second-hand illusions that always seem to vanish before we encounter them. Our call is to commit ourselves to the absolute God, to the one who Is. There is no ultimate evasion of the truth that we can only commit ourselves absolutely.

How do we learn commitment? What does Jesus tell us? He tells us to *worship*. The Hebrew word to worship derives from the root word, to *serve*. Jesus teaches us that 'The worshippers whom the Father wants must worship in spirit and truth.' The worshipper is one who serves, that is one who is absolutely at the disposition of his Lord. Absolutely. We must serve in spirit, that is from the depth of our being, not at the surface, not using other people's insights, but worshipping from the ground of our own experience, our own unique being. We must serve in truth, beyond all illusion, wholly accepting the reality of God and the reality of ourself as we are. The theological basis of Christian meditation is that the essential reality of prayer is the prayer of Jesus. In the same way that there is only one essential Christian prayer, the prayer of Christ himself, so there is only one Christian worship, the communion we have through Christ in the Trinitarian love. Each member of the Trinity wholly *at the service* of the other. Entry into this worship can only be found at the heart of creation, that is through the human worship of Christ, wholly at the disposition of the Father and receiving the Father's love, absolutely.

If we are to realize the full potential of the gift of life we need to see that our destiny is the same as Christ's. Our destiny is to be wholly at the service of God, to worship him in the depth of our being, to worship him in spirit and truth. Through such worship it is also our destiny to receive his love fully. The humble, ordinary task of saying the mantra, and saying it faithfully, is simply our way of entering this worship, of putting ourselves wholly at the disposition of God. Scripture returns again and again to the simplicity and clarity of the state of commitment and how far removed this state is from the mind-made substitutes of thought and language. It is when we learn to be simple that we enter into the absolute, the absolute commitment to the absolute love of God. To be simple is to be like Christ, an unambiguous *yes* to God.

> As God is true, the language in which we address you is not an ambiguous blend of Yes and No. The Son of God, Christ Jesus, proclaimed among you by us . . . was never a blend of Yes and No. With him it was and is, Yes. He is the Yes pronounced upon God's promises, every one of them. That is why, when we give glory to God it is through Christ Jesus that we say 'Amen'. And if you and we belong to Christ, guaranteed as his and anointed, it is all God's doing. It is God who has set his seal upon us, and as a pledge of what is to come he has given us the Spirit to dwell in our hearts. (2 Cor. 1:18–22)

Meditation is our total openness to the Spirit, so that in the whole of our life we say *yes* to God, say it with commitment, with generosity, absolutely.

Wholehearted in Christ

The modern person is characterized by a hungry search for wholeness. But what we have to learn is that the search will be fruitless without the commitment, the faith that is whole-heartedness:

> Whatever you are doing put your whole heart into it, as if you were doing it for the Lord and not for men, knowing that there is a Master who will give you your heritage as a reward for your service. (Col. 3:23–4)

Put your whole heart into it. Meditation calls us to the deepest and clearest level of understanding. Once we begin to meditate, once we have taken the first step, we soon realize that we can no longer remain in the shallows. The call we have responded to is for a complete reorientation of our being, a radical conversion. The call is, above all else, to enter the mystery itself, to learn what cannot be learned anywhere else or in any other way. For this call to be answered, every part of our being has to be involved because the knowledge we come to in meditation is not of a partial or quantative type. It is not that we know more and more *about* God, or that we know God to be all good, all holy, all just, all merciful and so on. On the contrary, in meditation we come to realize that we know as a consequence of being known. This is not easy either to believe or to understand at first, but we need only remember that in meditation we are entering into the basic relationship of our life. God, our Creator and our Father, calls us into an intimacy with him that arises because God first knows and loves us. And, in this act of knowing and loving us, God invites us to come into a relationship of knowing and loving him.

As I have suggested before it is not at all that we just know

97

more *about* God. We may indeed come to know more, especially as the relationship between our own experience and scriptural revelation matures. But instead of just knowing that God is all good, all wise, all merciful, all holy and always trying to add to this catalogue, we grow to know with certain silent knowledge that God is all in all. The knowledge that we come to in meditation is unshakable. It is rooted in inner experience and so meditation does not give rise to new information about God. It brings us into context with him. In meditating we find God as we find ourselves and as we find each other, each in our own place and each contributing to the other as we are, each in our own unique context.

Knowing the context in which we live is of supreme importance because only then are we constantly sensitive to our surroundings, to the ambience within which we have our being, within which we live. In meditating we learn to be more and more sensitive to God's presence which we now apprehend not as something external to us, but as something interior, something which grasps us by the roots. We go on to live in his presence with absolute confidence and with a growing sense of certainty that he is the rock, the foundation, on which we are securely founded. God is the ground of being in which we are eternally rooted. The longer we meditate the more we realize how unshakable faith is. It cannot be set aside simply because it is the very ground out of which we have learned to live. All this arises from the simple practice of saying our mantra every morning and every evening, in growing simplicity, in growing humility, in growing love, in growing wonder.

It is very easy for this to sound arrogant. It may seem extraordinarily arrogant to say that we come to know Christ as we persevere in our meditation. But I think the truth is not less than this. We do indeed come to know what it is to be in his presence. We do indeed learn, from being in his presence, to live out of the resources of that presence, thereby to communicate his goodness, his holiness to everyone we meet. We also come to understand that presence as present love, as actual compassion, as real understanding, as immediate forgiveness. The wonder of it all is that, if we live our lives rooted in these realities, as truths that are quite unshakable, we cannot be uprooted ourselves once the process is underway. Indeed, we are constantly deepening our commitment to Christ.

Now how does all this come about? Simply by learning to forget ourselves, by launching out into the depths of the reality of God as revealed in Christ. Saying the mantra loosens the root of the ego within us. It breaks up the ground that imprisons us in isolation, the bonds that hold us isolated in our self-preoccupation. And instead of self-fixation we are rooted in Christ. We learn to stand tall in his reality, to be one with him. But we have to put our whole heart into it. The 'heritage' St Paul speaks of is simply the right, the possibility to live the Christ-life, to be with Christ in our world; to be rooted as he is rooted in the Father. The way is the way of self-forgetfulness, the way of faithfulness, the way of simplicity. It is the way of holiness and the way of unknowing.

God Incarnate

When we are preparing for Christmas, we should try to reflect in the light of meditation about the essential, the spiritual significance of the Incarnation. God became Man so that Man might become God. This theme is the constant conviction of the Eastern Churches and the teaching of the Greek Fathers.

By the Incarnation God has touched our lives in Jesus, and the great importance of the feast of Christmas is that it is the celebration of our humanity, redeemed by being touched by God. God assumes the mortality of the human condition in Jesus so that we can burst through the bonds of death in him. Indeed, he bursts through all the chains that keep us bound by the earth. What we learn from his life is that the destiny of each one of us is to begin to live our lives fully now, in our present earthly, mortal condition. To live our lives now, as free men and women, not bound by fear or enchained by desire, but utterly in harmony with the liberating power of God's own energy. This energy of God cannot be bounded by any human limitation. It is the eternal life-source, not just constantly renewed in each one of us but always expanding in each one of us. And our invitation, our destiny, is to place our lives in complete harmony with this divine energy. And so, the Christian experience cannot be contained by any set of propositions, by any library of books, by any formulas or any creeds. It can only be adequately expressed in the human experience of Jesus himself. He alone, of all human beings, was able to say of God, 'Abba, Father'.

The mystery of the Incarnation and the sheer wonder of the Christian proclamation of truth is that Christ shares his experience with each one of us. And he actively invites each one of us to enter into his own experience of the Father. He

100

invites us not just to make some sort of intellectual assent or volitional intention. He invites us to *share*, to share with his experience in all its fullness, to share and to be carried away by the infinite thrust of his energy as he knows the Father and loves the Father, and as he in his turn is known and loved infinitely. And this is what we are called to. Every one of us.

In meditation we develop full attention, full commitment because what we set out for is to enter the eternal moment of God's self-communication in Jesus. We are called not just to consider this but to share it, to enter into it at the very depth of our being. And the result for us is deep, supreme, unshakable joy. Our minds and hearts are expanded beyond all isolation into oneness, into union. The Way is the way of daily fidelity.

Wherever we are on the path – whether we are just beginning and meditating twice every day for twenty minutes, or whether we have been on the path for some time and we meditate for thirty minutes or meditate three times a day – wherever we are, all that is required is that we give ourselves totally *now* to our commitment. It seems, when we begin, that this is asking a lot, but the feast of Christmas reminds us that God in his gift to us does not just give us a lot, he gives us everything of himself, in Jesus. Somehow we must understand that and we must understand it in the silence of our own heart. We must understand it in the eternal silence of God.

And so when we meditate each morning and evening, we each of us receive, as fully as we are now able to, the gift of God in Jesus. To receive it requires a generosity on our part that is not less than the generosity of God. That is why we must say our mantra with the greatest attention we can, with the greatest love we can. The words of Jesus constantly inspire us to deepen our generosity:

Father, I desire that these men who are thy gift to me, may be with me where I am. So that they may look upon my glory, which thou hast given me because thou didst love me before the world began. O righteous Father, although the world does not know thee, I know thee and these men know that thou didst send me. I made thy name known to them and will make it known so that the love thou hadst for me may be in them, and I may be in them. (Jn. 17:24–6)

Thought, Feeling, Love

Week by week, in the Tuesday night meditation groups at the Priory, I have tried to share with people something of the interiority of meditation and the way this interiority transforms the outreach dimensions of life through the experience of union. There is not a great deal we can say about it. But if there is anything we can say it is that it is the way to clarity of vision, and this is so because it is the way of love. To be in love is to see clearly and feel everything illuminated by love. Everything is shot through with the enlightening power that love unleashes. The call of Jesus to each one of us to follow him, living our lives out of this love means a growing in clarity, with depth and interiority of perception. The call of Christianity is to go beyond all obscurities and double focus, and to do so purified by the love of Jesus. The real call to each one of us is, therefore, to know ourselves as *being in love*. To see clearly is to know that the love of Jesus, the power of his purifying energy, is released and working in our hearts. The trouble is that when we think of our inner lives, of the 'life of the spirit', we tend to think of it in terms of thought and emotion. But religious thought and religious feeling have a very limited power to propel us beyond ourselves into the selflessness of love. Thinking and feeling are, I'm afraid, likely to lead us back always to imagination, the greatest enemy of the *reality* of Christ's presence in our hearts.

The spiritual life that is based on *thought* alone is likely to be as dry as dust. The spiritual life based on *emotion* alone is likely to lead us to the sort of religious intolerance that arises when our feelings escape from their moorings. Our call is to be rooted and founded in *love*.

Of course, thought and feeling are essential elements in every

103

pilgrimage; but the call of Jesus, to each of us, is to pass beyond them to the reality of God's all-powerful, ever-loving presence in our hearts. What we have to discover in meditation, and what each of us, I think, *must* discover if we are to live our lives to the full, is that the reality of God is the only foundation we can build on. Any thought of God, any emotion concerning God is subject to the shifting sands of our impermanent levels of consciousness. Meditation is the awakening to the reality of God at that level in ourselves where we do not have a shrine-image of him or a cult-devotion to him, but where God is, in his pure and gracious self-giving. This presence is the only ultimate sanity because God is the only ultimate reality. In God alone can we find uncompromising gentleness. In God alone can we find the courage to see what is to be seen, to travel the road we must travel. In God alone can we find the strength to take up our cross. And in God alone can we find that cross to be a burden sweet and light.

In the overall course of our life's pilgrimage we do not reject thought, we do not reject emotion, but we recognize that if the pilgrimage is to bring us to the fulfilment of God's pure Being, we must transcend them by a discipline that becomes, like the burden, sweet and light. Our meditation is that discipline. We do not think about God; we do not analyse our feelings about him when we are meditating. We say our mantra with absolute confidence, with absolute faith because we are in the presence of absolute Love. As a result, in our meditation thought is clarified because it is founded on the rock who is Christ and not on our egos. Our emotion, too, is purified and pacified by his gentleness, by his forgiveness, by his love. I think the importance of all this is that this clarity and purity free us for the greatest act of fraternal love of our life which is to lead others to this purity of consciousness, to this clarity of vision. Nothing that any of us could do for our neighbour could be greater than this service of leading them to realize their enormous potential, if only they can clarify their consciousness in Christ's. If only they can purify their emotion in the warmth of his love.

We must never forget the discipline of the way. There is no instant formula. We must say our mantra with ever *greater* faithfulness. We must return to our meditation with ever greater love. In these words from the letter to the Hebrews you can see the context of our meditation.

> But now Christ has come, high priest of the good things already in being, and the tent of his priesthood is a greater and more perfect one, not made by men's hands, that is not belonging to the created world. The blood of his sacrifice is his own blood and thus he has entered the sanctuary once and for all and secured an eternal deliverance. How great is the power of the blood of Christ, who offered himself without blemish to God, a spiritual and eternal sacrifice. And his blood will cleanse our conscience from the deadness of our former ways and will fit us for the service of the living God. (Heb. 9:11–14)

Meditation is our entry into that reality of Christ risen from the dead. Christ, by his power, fits us for the service of the living God.

Questions and Responses

Q: You sound impatient about communicating this teaching. How do you explain that? Shouldn't we leave it to God to persuade people?

A: Yes, I think that the impatience that I feel is that there seem so few who are on the Way. But I think that you are perfectly right: the timing is God's and once we realize that he calls us, basically what we can do is to say our mantra. There is nothing much else we can do apart from that. We cannot begin to tear our lives apart and try to restructure them. That leads to disaster for us and for others. We *can* say our mantra and we can follow the gift that is given to us from then on. But I think all of us need to feel a certain impatience or urgency, if that is a better word. Because the body of Christians as a whole, the body of the world as a whole, is so slow even to start on the Way and is so distracted by totally frivolous things. What I was saying, in so far as I was being critical of any of it, was simply that we foolishly postpone starting. The important thing is to start.

Q: I think an analogy would be a biblical line, 'Let your light so shine before men'. That tends to express the experience of the presence of God you speak of in a way that has it, somehow, show through you. Would it help to see it that way?

A: Yes, I think so, I don't think we have to go down to an electrical store to get a plug and put ourselves in the socket. I think that what is important is to have men and women of *growing* maturity. That is what St Paul is talking about and that maturity or wholeness is in Christ. That is the urgent thing. That is what calls for our involvement, our *engagement* in

French. I think we should really be *engagé* in that process. Just as one just person will save a city so I think that one person 'on the pilgrimage' can save a city. I think this is what we have to do in our own lives. Each of us must be prepared to be that one person. That is the basis of commitment for an authoritative community, a true Church. We also need to be aware of our responsibility to hand on the tradition. It can be handed on in various ways. St Paul says, 'some of us are teachers, some preachers. . .'. As meditators we do hand it on, principally through the effect that meditation has in our lives, as you rightly say. We must all sense the urgency that is involved. St Paul says, 'these are evil times'. We are still living in a world based on a power structure that is very fragile and totally unchristian. We have really got to develop that urgent sense of the importance of being on the Way.

Q: What does the word mean?

A: *Maranatha* means 'Come, Lord'. You can use another mantra but the word, the mantra, that I recommend you to use is *maranatha* to begin with. I think it is important to use it, if you can.

The essence of the mantra, as I have suggested to you, is that it brings you to silence. It is not a magic word. It is not a word that has any esoteric properties to it or anything like that. It is simply a word that is sacred in our tradition. *Maranatha* is possibly the oldest Christian prayer there is after the Our Father. It is a word that brings us to great peacefulness, to rest and calm. Certainly to begin with I would recommend you to use a word that has at least an open 'a' vowel sound in it. I think that everything considered the best word you could use to start with is *maranatha*.

Q: Are you supposed actually to see the light?

A: No, that is just a figurative expression.

Q: What happens if you do?

A: Ignore it. What you may find when you are beginning to

meditate is that all sorts of psychical phenomena are present. For some people, those who might like to think of themselves as more normal, nothing at all happens. Other people, maybe those who have more imagination or a stronger psyche or something else, will sometimes see colours or cloud formations or particular images. Or they will hear beautiful singing or harmonies, but the important thing is to go straight through all these phenomena. They are not at all important in themselves. They are much more likely to be associated with your liver and what you had for supper than with any deep spiritual experience. Not everyone likes to hear this, of course. But the important thing is to say the mantra in a growing spirit of poverty and fidelity.

Q: Can you say the mantra while still thinking of other things?

A: It is quite possible, even likely, that this happens. But, insofar as you can, very gently say the mantra and let go of the other things, without using force. The essence of meditation is that it is a way of great gentleness. You don't attempt, as it were, to hit the other thoughts over the head so as to banish them. You simply attend to the mantra more faithfully and let the other thoughts go. You may not be able to prevent them coming but you can let them go. You will find that you can't learn to meditate in a matter of days or weeks. Generally speaking the first twenty years are the most difficult! The important thing, though, is not how long it takes, nor how easy or difficult it is. The important thing is just to *be* on the Way. This is what changes everything.

Q: You say to leave the past behind when we meditate. But how can we do that when we are so conditioned by the past. What is the difference? What is the past?

A: I think the past is everything that has constituted your pilgrimage until that moment. I think one of the most difficult things for us to understand about meditation is the poverty of it, that we must, as it were, come naked into the presence of God each time we enter into the experience of it. What we want to do is very human, to try to bring our experience with us so we will be able to judge this new experience in the light of the past. But I think what we have to do, and this is what I mean in this context, is to accept that every time we sit down to meditate we are left just with our mantra; and with what *The Cloud of Unknowing* calls 'the naked intent upon God'. There is nothing else. We surrender everything. The past is there. You are there. But what I am saying is that we surrender that past entirely into the hands of God. We say, 'As of now I come to you as I am, naked, totally at your disposition and I surrender the past entirely into your hands.' Does that make it clear?

Q: Yes. One other thing you said also helped, 'You don't judge this new experience by the past and therefore it is better to have the past out of it.' It's very simple, in fact, isn't it?

A: The past must be set right aside to give us the simplicity that we need for the pilgrimage. That is part of the whole thing. It is like a child coming open-eyed to an experience and, therefore, able to come to it with wonder. I was with some children on Saturday morning and we were doing a little play together but we were rather short of props. I felt around and I had a comb in my pocket and I said, now, look at this comb. It is a golden comb and it possesses a marvellous power: every time you do your hair with it, it makes your hair golden too. One of the little boys jumped up and said, 'Hey, give me that comb. I've always wanted to have golden hair.' He was able to enter into the experience directly. I think that is really what we need in meditation.

Q: What about the sense of boredom? Should I feel worried if it seems nothing is happening in my meditation?

A: Well, no. But I think it is a real problem for Western people who are starting to meditate. But you will find that the practice is self-authenticating. I suppose if someone always felt completely bored while they were meditating, they would give it up. They wouldn't stay with it, they just could not persevere with it. In a sense, we expect it to be boring. You know there was a cartoon in the *New Yorker* of two monks meditating and one was saying under his breath to the other, 'What happens next?' and the other chap says, 'What do you mean, what next? This is it!'

But I think you will find that as you enter into the peace of it and the simplicity of it and the silence of it, it is anything but boring. What I would say to anyone who does at times find it boring is to persevere, keep going. *The* advice that I would give anyone is 'say your mantra'. That is perhaps the most difficult thing to understand when you are beginning. Because you think you should be 'praying' or you think you should be getting great insights or you should be levitating or you should be doing something, whereas the real thing is to say your mantra and to be *content* to say it. That is difficult. I think you have a good point in that it is particularly difficult for modern people because we are not a contented generation. We are always expecting something to happen. It seems that if we have a certain input then there will be a certain output, there will be a pay off. But that is why I say at the beginning: meditation is the way of unlearning and you have to unlearn both your materialistic attitudes and most of your religious attitudes as well. Both have to be unlearned. We are realizing what has happened and is happening eternally. The realization is what is happening in our meditation. When we see that there is no more boredom!

Q: My thoughts seem to be coming from all over the place and so if you cannot help but get distracted isn't it alright to let the mantra go?

A: Well, the great principle is 'pray as you can and not as you can't!' If the only way you can find peace is by standing on your head at that moment it would be probably advisable to stand on your head. But the advice that I would give you is, try, to the very best of your ability, to just keep saying the mantra. It seems much more difficult than it is. It is like swimming or riding a bicycle. You know when you see a bicycle for the first time as a child you look at it in awe and you think it is impossible, no one could possibly stay on those two wheels and keep going. I am bound to fall off. And you get on the thing and tense every muscle in your body and – you fall off. So you say, there you are, what did I tell you, it's impossible. It is the same with meditating. We tend to approach it from a very tense starting-point. But if you can only stay there, the gentleness and the compassion and the peace and the love of God will overwhelm you. You need not be at all concerned about your distractions. They are only a cause for humility. It is an extraordinary thing – here we are, living in the most sophisticated, complex culture that has been known on the face of the earth – with all the advantages we have of education, and every kind of book at our fingertips – and we cannot sit still for ten seconds! So it should make us humble. Just persevere with that encounter with humility and say your mantra. You have to be gentle when you start. But what I would suggest is, if you do find that you have to give up, say in the first week of meditating, well, maybe you had better give up. But in the second week, out of the seven days, only give up on six, not on all seven, and gradually try to extend it. Do not give up because you do not achieve perfection. Perfection is relative. You are perfect if you reach the potential you have at this moment. To be perfect means encountering our limits and gradually pushing them back.

Q: Is there a best time in the morning and in the evening?

A: The best time varies very much according to the body chemistry of the individual. The best time for most is probably early in the morning, before breakfast, when you are at your freshest. Perhaps a cold shower might be part of the prescription. And then in the evening, I think probably the best time is before your evening meal. That isn't always possible for everybody, especially if you are coming home from work and your family has got the meal ready or a guest arrives. It depends very much on the circumstances of your life. Those are probably the optimum times but what is of supreme importance is that you do meditate every morning and every evening. It can be done. The busiest people often find the time that the less busy say they cannot find.

111

Q: Would it matter if you changed the time from day to day? If you had to?

A: If you had to, not at all. No, the really critical thing is to put in those two meditations. When I was in Ireland a while ago I met a priest friend of mine who started to meditate about six years ago. He told me that when he started, he listened to what I had to say and said, 'Well, you know, this guy is a monk and has nothing to do all day but sit around. It's very easy for him to meditate twice a day, but I'm a busy parish priest. Therefore, I will read his signal: for *me*, "once a day".' And so, he said, for about a year he meditated once a day. Then he felt, 'You know, this is not working.' And he came to me to complain about it. And I said, 'Well, it's extraordinary. You meditate every morning and every evening, do you?' He said, 'Well, no, just the morning.' So I said, 'Well, you meditate in the evening as well and then we'll listen to the complaints.' And he did. He said that he could not describe to me the qualitative difference. He began his day and, as it were, prepared for his day out of that peace and inner rootedness in his essential being. And then he brought the whole day together at the end, as it were, gathering all the strands into the same essential reality. He said that the difference was astonishing to him. And he said, 'You know, I'll meditate every day, twice a day, for the rest of my life now, if I possibly can.'

Q: What about more than twice a day? Say, three? Or should we stick to just the two?

A: What I would recommend you to do when you are starting is to start with a morning and an evening meditation. When you have got that absolutely, regularly built in, then if you wanted to and if the circumstances of your life permit, put in a mid-day meditation. I think that would be good, but I wouldn't expect most people to come to that for maybe a couple of years or so. One has to start very gently, being very compassionate towards oneself. All of us I think find that we start, we give up, we start again, we give up and so on. You have to be very gentle, prudent and self-understanding. What I think you will find is that the experience itself is self-authenticating. Experience teaches. You will simply find that the longer you have been meditating for, the more your day seems to come into shape and the more purpose you have in your life. Then the more you begin to see the meaning in everything and the more you will find that love grows in your heart. Now it may be that there is a good deal of meanness there as well, but the love is growing. And that is the real test of meditation. But you cannot put any sort of materialistic test to meditation. More does not necessarily mean better. The real test is the love growing in your heart.

Religious Love

This is an example of St Paul's insight into the new life of the Christian experience:

> Formerly, you were yourselves estranged from God, you were his enemies in heart and mind and your deeds were evil. But now by Christ's death in his body of flesh and blood, God has reconciled you to himself, so that he may present you before himself as dedicated, without blemish and innocent in his sight. Only you must continue in your faith, firm on your foundations, never to be dislodged from the hope offered in the gospel which you heard. (Col. 1:21–3)

The great religious question that all of us have to face, and which I feel is the great question of our time, is how can each of us find our way into the *essential* Christian experience. How can we really enter into our faith as something utterly, presently real, something that we know not just as ideal, poetic, admirable or perfect but something we can recognize as essential? Essential in itself and therefore essential *for* us. In other words, we have to come to see our spiritual development as integral to our way of living. It is no exaggeration to say that unless we live our faith within the knowledge of Christ, we know nothing of essential value. And unless we live by being enlivened with his life, then we have not lived fully. And this is the heart of the Christian mystery. It is not about conceptual knowledge in the first instance, but about lived faith revealing the divine life of God. What St Paul was proclaiming was fullness of life, limitless life, 'eternal life'. Everything else, moral or dogmatic, in Christianity flows straight from that. And, without that source in the life force of the essential experience, all religious knowledge and all religious practice is lacking the essential

114

element. It is lifeless religion. It is abundantly clear from the teaching of Jesus and from the apostles' understanding of that teaching that his call is for our lives to be united in his life. The call is to union, to undifferentiated oneness. Uniting with him we pulsate with his life and, once the union is accomplished, when all egotistical retention and aggression is silenced, nothing can ever rupture it. As St Paul says, 'Who shall ever separate us from the love of Christ?'

One of the major contemporary problems Christianity faces is that so much theology is merely concerned with thoughts about God that are not derived from experience. These thoughts are in fact often divorced from experience of him by a rejection of the value of spiritual knowledge. The problem is not to abolish theology, of course, but to infuse spiritual life-experience into it so as to make it again a living theology that is generated by more than just the function of reflections on other reflections. True theology arises, too, from more than reflecting about other people's experience of God. Modern Christianity needs a strong, contemplatively generated theology which can engage the intelligence with all the ideas, problems and movements of modern consciousness. It must be more than reprocessed God-talk, human posturings in front of the Infinite. It must be God speaking in and through human experience, which is grounded in prayer. True theology is essential theology – much more, a reflection on the eternal Word of God, in the light of Jesus himself. True theology primarily depends not on knowing *about* words, but on knowing the Word. The first lesson we have to learn from prayer is that the Word is God (not words about God) and that God is Love. The whole of Pauline theology emphasizes that only knowledge that springs out of this experienced love has the power to redeem, to revitalize. This is what each one of us needs, to experience our redemption and to know that we are made free by grace and we are vitalized by that faith consciousness. Father Bernard Lonergan writes that faith is knowledge born of religious love.

By opening our hearts to love at the deepest and most silent level of our being, we are not repressing human knowledge or rejecting human values or relationships. On the contrary, all of these are enlightened, that is, we see them in a new light, in a transcendent light. We see a new light in them. The extraordinary thing about the Christian message is that this light is not less than the light of Christ, the light who is Christ. The call to us to enter this light is for each of us to know from our own experience, with St Peter and St Paul and St John, that we are not just reading poetry to each other or designing religious scenarios for dreamtime 'walkabouts'. They were trying to communicate to us the fact, the supreme and redeeming fact, that Christ's light shines in our heart and that the first task of our life is to be open to it, to be bathed in it, to be made whole in it and to see with it.

Meditation is our journey to that light. To come to it we have to learn how to be humble, to be patient and to be faithful. By faithfully returning to your meditation every morning and every evening you will learn all this. Reciting the mantra from the beginning to the end of your meditation you will learn humility. By the gift of God you will then learn of your own loveableness as you learn that the light shines *for you*. You will learn that the union, the oneness, is for you. And you will learn that in the union you are one with all. Meditation is so important because it leads us to our place in the divine plan, which is to be rooted and founded in Christ. We find Christ in our hearts and then we find ourselves in him and, in him, in all creation:

> He rescued us from the domain of darkness and brought us away into the kingdom of his dear Son, in whom our release is secured and our sins forgiven. He is the image of the invisible God, his is the primacy over all created things. . . . Through him God chose to reconcile the whole universe to himself, making peace through the shedding of his blood upon the cross, to reconcile all things, whether on earth or in heaven, through him alone. (Col. 1:13–15, 20)

The invitation to meditate is to enter into the truth of that reunion, or reconciliation. To accept it is to rejoice in our reconciliation, in Christ, with Christ, through Christ.

The Way who is Christ

We will meet with fewer difficulties as we meditate if we approach it from the beginning with the right understanding. Words can clarify or confuse and seeing a shared meaning can be difficult, but we need to use the appropriate words to get the understanding straight from the beginning. We are unclear if we think of meditation, for example, as a technique. In the modern world, we are conditioned to thinking about techniques. Life presents us with a series of problems, each of which needs a specialized technique to solve it. People sometimes say to me, what is the technique that you teach? But what I want to suggest to you, right at the beginning of your own pilgrimage, is that meditation is not really a technique at all. It is much more a *way*. In essence, it is the Way that is Christ, who said of himself, I am the Way. In meditation we follow a way to be as open as we can be in this world, with our limitations, to his spirit within us. To be truly open to anything calls for discipline, for devotion, for dedication. To be open to his Spirit is to practise the discipline of a disciple who never forgets that he is the Way.

For modern people the word meditation often suggests passivity or inaction, but it is neither of these. Meditation is the way to a fulfilled state of being. Indeed it is the state of being which is prior to all action and without which all action will tend to be shallow, without the significance of permanence. All sane action in our lives must flow out of being at one with being. This means that to meditate, we begin to learn to be wholly alert; to accept oneself wholly; to love oneself; and to know oneself rooted and founded in the utter reality that we call God.

For the greater part of our life we live at the surface level,

117

so often reacting off immediacy. But in meditation we are not reacting to external stimuli. We are learning to live out of the depths of our being, where we are finding and responding to the supreme, sole stimulus, the Creator. We are learning to be the person that we are called to be, as we align ourself in response to that source which has called us into existence. Being the person we are means enjoying the gift of our own creation before and beyond all desire, all expectations, all demands. The early monastic Fathers described this state as the state wherein we are one, and beyond all desire because we are utterly filled with the fullness of God. Being one is being whole. We have all we need for oneness, for wholeness, for passing beyond all desire. Desire is undesirable because it can only complicate and divide what is meant to be simple and unified.

The experience of meditation is therefore the experience of simplification, learning to become ever more and utterly simple. This is the secret of all happiness; to enjoy what is. Being is the primal experience of us all. Prior to all having, prior to all doing, being is enduring. It is the eternal in each of us.

Now let me remind you of the way of being. You must learn to be still, to be simple, to be one. And the way that the monastic tradition gives us is the way of the mantra, constantly repeating it in our heart. However many talks you may listen to on meditation, or however many books you may read – and I do not recommend you read too many or listen to too many talks – I would urge you always to remember this. The tradition is crystal clear to us now, from our own experience. You may know this already from your own experience: that to be still, to be silent and to be simple comes as you learn to be faithful to the recitation of the word, from the beginning to the end. If you discover that you are not saying it, start saying it again gently, simply, humbly, faithfully. And keep on returning to it from the beginning to the end. Do not think about it, do not think about anything. Listen to it. Listen to the sound of it. The mantra is just like a harmonic, and when we listen to that harmonic sounding in our own heart we gradually and simply come into harmony throughout our own being and so into harmony with all creation, and into harmony with God.

Meditation is the way that is entirely open to God because it is entirely open to our own being and to the whole of creation. The Way is a free flowing way and it flows with the power of God that we discover in the depths of our own being. In that power, with that power and through that power we come to meet God in creation. So what is there that is passive about meditation? Meditation is learning to live out of the fullness of power. That power is the life of God and it is the power of Love.

Never forget the essence of the way, reciting your word in ever deepening humility and ever deepening faithfulness, no thoughts, no imagination, no image. Be faithfully on the Way, the Way who is Christ. And be prepared for the awakening that St Paul describes as the essence of Christian faith:

> I pray that the God of our Lord Jesus Christ, the all glorious Father, may give you the spiritual powers of wisdom and vision by which there comes the knowledge of him. I pray that your inward eyes may be illumined so that you may know what is the hope to which he calls you, what the wealth and glory of the share he offers you and how vast the resources of his power, open to us, who trust in him. They are measured by his strength and the might which he exerted in Christ, when he raised him from the dead. (Eph. 1:17–20)

Sit down, be still in body and still in spirit. Recite your word and be open to that power as and when it is revealed to each of us.

Past, Future and the Present

Meditation is experientially concerned with two important things: the presence of God, and becoming attentive to that presence. These concerns are as ancient and as modern as human consciousness itself, and no life can claim to be fully human that does not incorporate some training and attention to them. To ignore or postpone them is the foolishness of sin. Wisdom is different:

> If it is your wish, my son, you can be trained. If you give your mind to it you can become knowledgeable; if you enjoy listening, you will learn; if you become attentive, you will become wise. (Si. 6:32–4)

The purpose of meditation is that we listen and that we become attentive. We become attentive to the presence of God, who described himself in the definitive Old Testament revelation as *I Am* Who Am. Isaiah, who gives us the name of the Messiah, calls him Emmanuel, *God with us*. Over and over in the biblical revelation we read of how God reveals himself to those who walk with him, to those who live 'in confidence in his sight'. Again this is what our meditation is essentially about: a *being with God* who is with us and making the journey of transformation confidently in his care. Meditation is a pilgrimage in which we journey to our own heart, there to find Jesus – the revealer and embodier of God. Finding his Spirit is the first stage of our pilgrimage. Then we continue our pilgrimage with Jesus to the Father.

The preliminary stage is the journey to our own heart. It enables us to discover for ourselves the truth that St Paul puts before us in the letter to the Corinthians.

Surely you know that you are God's temple, where the Spirit
of God dwells. (1 Cor. 3:16)

Each of us is invited to that self-knowledge for ourselves. It is
not enough to know it in somebody else's witness; we must
know it through the living word of God as it dwells in our
hearts. But we do not know this through our own power; we
know it through his self-revealing power. It is this power that
is revealed in us when we become silent and attentive.

Every year in the liturgy of Holy Week, we listen to the
historical narratives of our salvation. We read and ponder them
throughout the year. It is very important for us to understand
that the essence of religion is not found in the *memory* of these
past events. The heart of true religion is *making present* the
moment of salvation. The truly religious moment is a trans-
temporal moment. The religious moment is the eternal now of
the God who is 'I Am'.

As an idea, the present moment has little power to redeem
us. We need the training, the total listening the Book of
Wisdom speaks of, to make the idea a redemptive experience.
Meditation is this training. Meditation is our availability to the
eternal moment. In it, during the chronological time of our
meditation, we are, in so far as we can be, wholly present to
the God who is. From our point of view, in our meditation we
are with *him*. *God with us*, Jesus, reveals the glory of the
Father to us in our own hearts. Purifying our hearts for the
reflection of this glory is the whole purpose of the mantra. The
mantra trains us to listen and so brings us to fullness of being,
to God, in the present moment as we leave the past entirely
behind and place the future in the hands of God. In our meditation we are not thinking about the past, nor planning for the
future because we are open to the eternal moment, the eternal
now of God. Here is the importance of the mantra, in that it
puts an end to thinking of the past, of the future, and leaves
us wholly open to the presence of the God who is.

Meditation is therefore a way of renunciation. Being so, it is
also a way of discipline, an ascetical path. All this, renunciation,
discipline, ascesis is caught up and combined in the act of faith
that is the mantra, always growing as we learn to say our

121

mantra with deeper fidelity. On Good Friday we come to see Jesus emptying himself completely and utterly in faith. The Cross is Jesus totally dispossessed and through this total poverty of pure faith he reveals the glory of the Father. It is the same with each of us. We must dispossess ourselves so that the glory of Jesus may have full power to shine in each one of us and may come to full brilliance. Jesus is the Word of God, and in the Word, God is revealed. Our little word of faith, too, is our way to the revelation of God in Jesus within our own hearts. Jesus is the Word spoken out of the eternal silence of God. Jesus is the Word who summons us into that eternal silence of God. 'Surely you know that you are God's temple, where the Spirit of God dwells.'

This is what we *must* know. We are meant to know with the certainty of faith, the certainty that comes from the presence we apprehend in our own hearts. A presence that is now, that is eternal. The universal Way is the way of poverty. As St John of the Cross puts it: 'The way of possession is the way of dispossession.' The universal Way is the way of fidelity. We are faithful each time we meditate. The Way is Jesus and each of us learns directly by participation from his poverty, from his dispossession and from his fidelity. His humanity is the road we travel.

There can be no other foundation beyond that which is already laid, I mean Jesus Christ, himself. . . . Surely you know that you are God's temple where the Spirit of God dwells. (1 Cor. 3:11, 16)

Redemptive Love

All generations articulate differently the problems from which they suffer or the fears that perplex them. But all times have aspired to the condition of unity as the state of completion and peace. The most essential quality of Christian faith that needs to be recovered and communicated today is its revealing of the key to unity.

> God has made known to us his hidden purpose, such was his will and pleasure, determined beforehand in Christ, to be put into effect when the time was ripe, namely that the universe, all in heaven and all on earth might be brought into a unity in Christ. (Eph. 1:9–10)

This is the eye of the Christian vision. It is a vision of transcendent unity. All humanity and creation united in Christ with the one Father is united with the One who is three in one. Everyone is seen achieving that inner harmony in themselves, so that within us there are no more seeds of division but only seeds of peace. A unity like this brings with it great peace and therefore great power. It is not force, but the power to meet life and to live human life to the full. In this vision, which is not at all an abstract vision, all matter in creation is drawn into this trans-figuring cosmic movement of unity and it achieves the final unity by entering fully into the unity of the divine harmony itself. It is very important, if we want to live our faith not just to think it, to remember that this is not just some beautiful theory. It is not an abstraction or projection of fantasies but it is a *call* to everyone of us to realize the deep, personal joy, the irreversible liberation that comes when we realize the grand design of which we are part. We taste peace when we realize that, in that grand design, everyone of us is called to fulfilment in the All, called to fulfilment by our own unity and our union with the One who is one.

Each of us must come to terms with this vision as much more than a theory but as something absolutely practical. That is the part that meditation plays. We are not meant to take St Paul's word for it alone, or to take anyone's word for it, but to enter into the reality ourselves. We are *meant* to experience it, and to do so by leaving our limitations behind. That is the real marvel of the vision proclaimed by Christ and by the early Church: that the way of self-transcendence is the way in which the Kingdom is realized, equally in each of us and in all of us together. But it is a demanding vision of absolute liberty of spirit. Our call is the challenging call to wholeness, to oneness, to union. Also, we come to see that our call is to communicate this by our life. To live it entails the responsibility to communicate it to others, but we can only communicate it if we fulfil the responsibility to become wholly ourselves, to realize our own destiny. This vision of unity is the vision that has inspired countless men and women over the ages to tread the path away from self, away from egoism, away from isolation and deep into the mystery of God himself. As I have said to you before, the call that each of us has summons us to an infinite expansion of spirit. But we cannot possibly respond to that call, we cannot enter into that vision without discipline, without commitment to the daily response.

When we sit down to meditate every morning and every evening, we respond to the task that is given to each of us to grow into that vision and into liberty of spirit, to advance in the infinite expansion of our consciousness in Christ.

St Paul speaks frequently of the evolving maturity of Christians. The call to prayer, the call to meditation is precisely a call to grow up, to leave the ego-centred irresponsibility of childishness behind and to become ourselves by finding ourselves *beyond* ourselves in union with the All. Again, understand that this requires a personal response, not just an agreeing nod, from each of us. The invitation is to see with our own eyes, to hear with our own ears and to love with our own hearts but also to do this in union with him who is Love. Now, in practice this requires of each of us to go beyond all our per-

sonal, historical dividedness. All the dividedness within ourselves is required to be transcended. All the barriers that separate us from our true selves and from others and from God must
be dismantled. And that means leaving all our images behind.
Images that we have of ourselves, the images that we have of
others and the images that we have of God. The Christian
vision requires us to be open to God at an imageless depth,
and it is in openness there that all the false dichotomies are
resolved in union, in oneness. In other words, the call is for us
all together to return to a fundamental simplicity. The call of
deep prayer is no less than the call to *be*, to be yourself, to be
in love, in trust, in total openness to what is. And it is almost
meaningless to say that God is Love until we know it for
ourselves, through an experience of our being in the being of
God. Our call is to know it and that is what Christianity is
about. Everything in Christianity must lead us to that or else
we are left with a receipt for deceit.

The vision itself is so intoxicating that we must approach it
with humility. We must learn to be truly humble, to know our
own place, and our place is to be rooted in what is now. We
must learn to be 'meek and humble of heart', and to know
what that means. Meekness and humility simply depend upon
opening our eyes to the vision of God, so that we know that
he is the centre of the universe, the centre of all creatures in
creation. He is the creator and we are creatures. Each of us
has our own unique essential place and part to play which is
our dignity and our burden. The only power that we can trust
absolutely is the power of the One who humbled himself absolutely. You only need to remember the death of Christ to enter
into this humility, because the essential message of the Cross
is the power of pure love, a power that arises from a total
selflessness. The crucifix is there to remind us of our call to
leave egoism behind and to understand otherness; to understand the power of pure love.

The one writing and the one reading are both redeemed.
Each one of us in whatever set of relationships we might
imagine, is redeemed, that is, delivered from our own ego by
love. Love alone has the power to redeem and absolute love
redeems absolutely. Now as we know, this power to know and

to love is to be found in our own hearts. And this is our pilgrimage, to our own hearts. The only thing necessary is that we seek this love with supreme seriousness, with generosity and with faithfulness. That we make that time available, every day of our lives, every morning and every evening in the quiet, in the hidden quiet of our own home, going to our own place of meditation to be silent; there to enter into the eternal reality of God, a reality that is to be found in our own heart. This is the only pilgrimage that is necessary. On it we find love, beyond all compromise, beyond all fear, beyond all timidity.

Let me remind you again because it is such a precious thing to know, that what we have to learn is the selflessness of saying the mantra. The selflessness of saying it from the beginning to the end of our meditation complements the selflessness required to get up that little bit earlier in the morning to meditate. And to meditate again in the evening, after a full day, when we are tired. To be generous enough to seek *the one thing* that is necessary. In that very act of seeking we discover the unity of which we are part, a unity of all in all.

Contemplation and Action

The chapters in this book are drawn from talks given to weekly meditation groups meeting at the Montreal Priory. On Monday nights the group is largely composed of new meditators, whom we recommend to come for ten weeks. Then they can join an ongoing group that meets on Tuesday nights which is composed of people who have begun to commit themselves to daily meditation. People often ask what is the difference between the Monday and the Tuesday night groups. If I explain that the Tuesday night group are the 'advanced' meditators they become more silent, more uneasy!

One of the essential things we need to remember at all stages of the spiritual journey is that we are not measuring progress in meditation. Indeed, I think it is impossible to measure progress as you would measure progress, for example, in the arts or in skills of language or learning to ride a bicycle. But a cautious comparison can be helpful. In fact meditating is very like learning to ride a bicycle. It is about direction and balance. As you know, in learning to ride a bicycle you need a certain amount of effort, but not too much. If you hang on too tightly, too stiffly, you will come off at the first corner. On the other hand, if you let go of the handle-bars altogether you will fall off even on the straight. So you require the same kind of finesse and flexibility in riding a bicycle as in learning to meditate. The mantra should not be used like a sledge hammer. You must learn the gentle art, the art of the delicacy of saying your mantra.

One of the reasons this is a valuable art to learn is that it prepares us for meeting our great opportunity as Christians, which is to respond in all situations of life, all moods, at every corner in our lives, to the gift that is given to us by God in

127

Jesus. It is a gift which the Church mediates, just as our bodies mediate us to other people, and this is why the Church is described as the Body of Christ. But it is not a stiff, inert body. It is a supple and conscious body. The call we hear in the Church is to become *fully* conscious. It is not a call to rest in its visible bodiliness, in its structures and organizations, but to become as free as the Spirit. This understanding of the Church helps us to see how we can describe God as pure consciousness, as Spirit. And so, the more we, as the Church, become conscious, the more godly we become, the more rooted in God.

One of the tensions that runs through the history of Christianity is a tension between the active and contemplative modalities. One of the tragedies of modern Christianity is that the tension has become so slack. Every Christian is called to live the contemplative dimension of the Christ-vision. Every Christian, in other words, is called to a deep *consciousness* of what it means to be created by God, of what it means to be redeemed by Jesus, of what it means to be a temple of the Holy Spirit. Whenever religious people have turned their backs on that contemplative dimension of their calling, they have become too *busy*, unreflectively active, and they usually end up by becoming busy-bodies. If our life is rooted in Christ, rooted in his love and the conscious knowledge of his love, then we need have no anxiety about regulating our action. Our action will always spring from and be informed and shaped by that love. Indeed, the more active we are, the more important it is that our action springs from and is grounded in contemplation. And contemplation means deep, silent, communion; knowing who we are. Knowing who we are by being who we are. That we are rooted and founded in Christ, the Resurrection of God, is Christian self-knowledge.

Every Christian is called to be a reincarnation of Christ. Every Christian is called to undertake the pilgrimage to their own heart of flesh and there to find the living Christ. In that awakening we know our own potential. We know we have the capacity to communicate Christ because when we discover him we will be *sure* we know him. And when we know ourselves so confidently in him, we cannot help communicating that knowledge, radiating that love. Every Christian is called to be a personal reincarnation and indeed that is the sense in which the Church is the Body of Christ, a body alive with and enlivened with his Spirit. But this requires consciousness. In his great sermon one Christmas morning in the fourth century, Pope St Leo cried out, 'O Christians, recognize your dignity. Know who you are. Know that you are the beloved of Christ.' Now meditation is our own commitment to that truth. We cannot rest content with just knowing this at the level of theory. We cannot be content knowing it only in terms of theological propositions. We must know it deeply and personally because it can only be known in any real sense at the level of personhood. The call is to communion with Jesus: your person open to his personal love.

The gift of his Spirit that is given to each one of us is infinite. It is the gift of the totality of God pouring out his Spirit into each of us and our response has to mirror that generosity and totality. It is a call to Christians *not* to respond mindlessly, half-heartedly, occasionally. The call is to respond generously with everything we are, with everything we have at this moment to bring to this response. And we have much to bring. We have our hearts, our minds, our lives, all of which, when we meditate, are integrated, concentrated and aligned on Christ. Everything that we are comes into a harmony with his being, with his love. Nothing is excluded and that is why we have to learn to say the mantra with such total fidelity, total generosity, total attention. The gift *is* given. All we have to do, each one of us, is to be open to it, to realize it. But we must approach our task and follow our way with simplicity, with humility and with gentleness. We must learn to be very gentle with ourselves as we learn to root the mantra in the heart. Only the smallest effort is required. Everything is given to us and basically what is asked of us is only that we are faithful to the daily pilgrimage and that we give the pilgrimage first place in our lives. Fidelity leads us to realize that the gift *is being* given. Then, as each morning and evening we turn faithfully to our meditation and during our meditation remain faithful to the mantra, the gift reaches us, the cycle is completed.

Do we do this just for ourselves? As you know the Church and the world are starved of wisdom and of love. In most places in the world the Churches are becoming beleaguered. In most places there is a deepening sense of ruin and of the absence of wisdom. But one wise man or woman can always hold back the flood. So there is no greater act of social or political or religious responsibility that any of us could undertake than to become more fully conscious, more fully rooted in consciousness, in God. Never let anyone discourage you on the path of meditation as in any way being in opposition or conflict with social, political or religious responsibility. The one thing that all societies need is wisdom. There is only one path of wisdom. And the fountainhead of wisdom is to be found in your heart, in the mystery of prayer.

> In the same way you must regard yourselves as dead to sin and alive to God, in union with Christ Jesus. Put yourselves at the disposal of God, as dead men raised to life, yield your bodies to him as implements for doing right; for sin shall no longer be your master, because you are no longer under Law but under the grace of God. (Rom. 6:11, 13–14)

Contact details for WCCM centres worldwide

International Centre
The World Community for Christian Meditation
St Mark's
Myddelton Square
London EC1R 1XX
UK
Tel: +44 20 7278 2070
Fax: +44 20 7713 6346
welcome@wccm.org
www.wccm.org

For countries not listed below contact the International Centre

Argentina	www.meditacioncristiana_argentina
Australia	www.christianmeditationaustralia.org
Belgium	www.christmed.be
Brazil	www.wccm.com.br
Canada	www.meditatio.ca
Chile	www.meditacioncristiana.cl
China	www.wccm.hk
Czech Republic	www.krestanskameditace.com
Denmark	www.kristenmeditation.org
Fiji	frdenise@connect.com.fj
France	www.meditationchretienne.org
Germany	www.wccm.de
Haiti	inobert@yahoo.fr
Hong Kong	www.wccm.hk

India Christian Meditation Centre	jpst_1995@yahoo.co.uk
Indonesia	www.meditasikristiani.com
Ireland	www.wccmireland.org
Italy	www.meditazionecristiana.org
Japan	www.esuk.net/wccm
Latvia	www.jesus.lv
Malaysia	wccm.malaysia@gmail.com
Malta	www.wccmalta.org
Mexico	www.meditacioncristiana.com
Netherlands	www.wccm.nl
New Zealand Christian Meditation Community	ccm@ihug.co.nz
Norway	www.norge@live.no
Philippines	czgomez123@yahoo.com
Poland	www.wccm.pl
Portugal	www.meditacaocrista.com
Singapore	www.wccmsingapore.org
South Africa	www.wccm.co.za
Spain	www.meditaciocristiana.cat/
Sri Lanka	aloma@dplgroup.com
Switzerland	deborah.walton@gmail.com
United Kingdom	www.christian-meditation.org.uk
USA	www.wccm-usa.org
Venezuela	www.meditadores.blogspot.com
Vietnam	tinvuicfc@gmail.com
West Indies	ruthsjc@wow.net